C000228373

One Woman's Journey

IN SEARCH OF
FREEDOM

Text © 1997 Eliza Forder
All rights reserved

No part of this publication may be reproduced, stored in a
retrieval system, or transmitted in any form or by any means,
electronic, mechanical, photocopying, recording or otherwise,
without the prior permission of the Copyright owner.

ISBN   0 9524677 1 2
Published by Usha Publications, Dent, Cumbria. LA10 5QL
Cover Design by Chris Miller
Typeset by Cypher Digital Imaging in Palatino
Printed and bound for Imago by
Biddles Ltd, Guildford and King's Lynn

Cover photographs: John Forder

One Woman's Journey

IN SEARCH OF
FREEDOM

USHA
PUBLICATIONS

AKNOWLEDGEMENTS

My deepest thanks go to Josie Dolan, my editor, whose love of words and profound spiritual understanding have been a constant source of inspiration during the past year. I am also indebted to Lynsey Beauchamp who originally spurred me on to write this book – without her encouragement it may never have been started. And once again I am grateful to John, my family, Val Corbett, and many other close friends for their continued support and valued criticism. They, as well as others, have helped make this book what it is.

Your own Self-Realization is the greatest
service you can render the world.

Sri Ramana Maharshi

Drops in the ocean. Is that what we are?

Imagine being caught inside one, bound by its unique sense of identity and form, and then remembering that the whole ocean is there if only we could get rid of the perimeter walls . . . the pain of separation begins to stir.

And to know that this infinitesimal drop is always a part of, and always subject to that surge and swell, the rising and falling . . . yes, those familiar feelings of vulnerability and fear come to the surface once more.

1

I had to run the race. I had no choice. I never wanted to compete for I knew I could never be the winner. Taunted by jibes from my peers, I took my place at the starting line – two six year old girls seeking to preserve themselves in the face of each other and their school friends. If I lost I would be jeered at, if I won I would be despised . . . for the other girl was undoubtedly the favourite.

'Ready, steady – go.'

I was small but agile and full of determination. I got off to a good start and found it difficult to hold myself back because my legs seemed to be carrying me so effortlessly. I could sense the tousled brown hair of my opponent slipping away behind me and realized that I was well ahead. I dreaded the comments lest I should win but I couldn't stop now – it was impossible to put on the brakes when I was running so well. The ridge that separated the gravel and the lawn loomed up in front of me. It signified the finish and suddenly I found myself aiming for it, filled with intent and new-found energy and no longer caring what the other children would say. Yes – I wanted to win, just for my own sake. I bounded home and collapsed on the grass in a heap, exhausted but pleased with my performance.

The face of a red-haired boy stared down at me hard as I gasped for breath.

'You're nothing. You cheated. You know what happens to cheats? Come on Mary, let's show her.'

The defeated girl and her freckled boyfriend tugged me toward a wooded area at the end of the school garden.

'We're going to tie you to this tree and pinch you 'til you say you cheated and you're sorry.'

The little boy, who seemed quite big to me, pulled some string out of his pocket and wound it around me several times until I was securely tied to the tree. Then the pinching, scratching and punching began. It was not hard, but hard enough to hurt inside. I did not want to let them see me suffer so I never shouted out. Instead I tensed my arms, bit my lip, felt my eyes sting but I held on tight. No tear was shed, no cry was uttered, no flinch was seen and, after a little while, they got bored.

'Come on, let's leave her. She's stupid anyway.'

And so the pattern of my youth was moulded. Success eluded me, outside pressures thwarted me, and I could not find a way out of my predicament. It seemed easier to retreat to an inner world and look for answers . . .

Among the middle-class élite of Cambridge life, restraint was normal. It was the probing of the mind that mattered, not understanding the emotions. The kindling of deeper feelings was inspired through art, literature and music, and my father was a lover of all three. An unseen Rembrandt would lure him across the world, a rare recording of a Bach cantata would be prized for his collection and, from Anthony to Lear, his love affair with the great bard supported him through each stage of his life. He also had a passion for botany. Above all the sedge family, or Carex, caught his imagination. 'With only eighty or so you can really begin to understand their habits, hybrids and idiosyncrasies.' And no bog or crag, no rain or mist, would deter him from searching out a particular plant. His gentle demeanour and breadth of vision ensured that he was a much loved and respected man. He had a handsome, rugged face and he was tall. When he lifted me up to give me a shoulder ride, I found his slow, rhythmic gait strangely comforting, and I loved the heightened vantage point of the world. When I put my arms under his chin and held on tight, I felt safe.

I was the youngest of four – two brothers and a sister – but we were rarely together as a family: the boys were sent to boarding-school at eight years old. The annual treat for my sister and me was to be dressed up in blue linen dresses and taken to see my brothers play in the school cricket matches. It was during the holidays we got to know them better. When the rain teemed we would play Bezique or poker, and if it was fine we would either create games in the garden using the swing, rope and trapeze, or resurrect the wooden platform in the walnut tree. Squatting up there and peeping out between the leaves, it was easy to create an imaginary world of my own. When I was able, I would take up scraps of food and cooking utensils so that I could play at being mother – this was my place of refuge.

Summers were spent at my grandmother's house in Cornwall. Our different ages and interests meant that for the most part we followed our own leisure pursuits. Some fished and sailed, while others picnicked, surfed and swam. They were lazy days but somehow the games seemed more real out there on the cliff tops with plenty of people to take part and the sea pounding away two hundred feet below. The cowboys bounded along the sea-sprayed turf full of bravado, shooting at every moving object in sight, while the Indians relied on stealth to lay siege to enemy territory. For them the skill of the game was to move forward without being seen, using the stone walls and gorse bushes for cover. As an Indian my deftness came into its own for I was determined to stay hidden and survive: that meant that I could stay in the game and, more than anything, I loved to play.

In our Cambridge circle, the emphasis was on academic achievement. The children of those who had already achieved intellectual excellence felt compelled to establish their own credentials in the world of 'gown'. But it was a competitive market place and one to which I was never inclined. I preferred to paint pictures in my mind and lose myself in a world of dreams. My mother, however, was a shrewd disciplinarian who recognized the importance of sharpening the senses and broadening the mind. She was a sociable lady with a socialist conscience, who believed in doing the best for her children as well as for the world. If I made mistakes at piano practice or with

French verbs, she would anger easily and then my nerves would make me fault more. I feared her wrath and wanted to please her and so, since I had more confidence with domestic tasks, I preferred to spend time cooking, cleaning and ironing. If I performed well I won her praise, and that was what I wanted more than anything else.

But too many times I had no chance of helping at all. During the holidays, it was arranged that I should go and stay with my godmother who sought companionship for her daughter who was my own age. It was a two-edged sword. I hated being sent away from home yet, because their family was wealthier than ours, I was treated to trips abroad that opened my eyes to different places and cultures. It was when I was staying at their country home near Cambridge that the head of the household, an eminent scientist, thought it his duty to test my level of intelligence. I shrank from such quizzing and wondered what it had to do with him.

'Bif.' It was the nick-name that he had given me. 'Why does a volcano erupt?'

I leaned against the French window, pressed my nose against the glass, and watched the shadows cast by the wisteria dance around the terrace. I did not feel like answering. The other adults in the room swallowed up the question and the conversation soon devolved around different kinds of earth movements, the ability to forecast their occurrence, and their effect on the population and environment. The sun bathed the garden with a warm evening glow and I noticed the croquet hoops set up on the lawn. I wanted to run out and hit a ball or two.

'Bif.' I was startled from my reverie by the penetrating voice of my friend's father. I knew that it was going to be difficult for me to escape this time.

'Look up the word 'seismology'. The dictionary is over there.'

At first I wasn't sure whether he was asking me for his sake or for mine. I followed the line of his finger and saw that he was pointing to a large bookcase at the end of the drawing-room. The bottom shelf was full of dictionaries and encyclopedias. My head dropped down as I slowly crossed the room staring at the blue-grey carpet in search of inspiration. The books seemed so big and overwhelming. I scanned the ten volumes in front of me while singing the alphabet inside my head. I could never remember the order of the rrs, sss and tts. After a while the appropriate volume stared back at me and I knelt on the floor to open it, feeling momentarily relieved. There were so many different words so close together, and the type was so small. I turned the pages slowly, not knowing whether I should be going forward or back. With all those letters to sort through, my mind could not focus – and there was that expectant silence in the room. I felt numbed. The print got smaller, my mind got more confused, and soon all I could see on the page was a grey blur where one letter merged into another.

'Well?' The voice boomed.

'I - I . . I . ' There was nothing to say for I had not found the word.

Yet in that stutter – in that moment – a thought of such precision pierced my mind that the clouds of confusion started rolling back, sweeping away the dross.

I realized something that he did not. I knew that what he had asked me to do was stupid. I recognized it and he seemed oblivious to it. There was no point in showing me up in front of those people. It did not teach me anything. No one felt comfortable, and I doubted that he had gained much satisfaction from watching me stumble. But he was blind to this and I saw it – even though I was only eight years old. The page came back into focus. I sorted out my alphabet, found the word, and said its meaning disinterestedly.

In that instant I recognized the difference between being clever and being wise – and I knew that what I wanted was wisdom. A spark ignited inside me and I did not want it to be extinguished by the world of head games that surrounded me. How was it possible to deepen one's understanding of human nature, life and its meaning? I was still so young yet I was curious to know more . . .

I lied when I said that I did not mind going to boarding-school.

I was only ten and I minded desperately. But I knew what was expected of me and I did not want to fail my parents. Despite my feelings of fear and apprehension it seemed safer to keep quiet. I kept reminding myself that the family I was reluctant to leave behind was a figment of my imagination anyway. My father was working in London, my brothers were away, my sister had her own friends and my mother was busy with local council and judicial affairs.

There were few conversation pieces between my mother and me as we drove to Bristol in the old Humber car. I wore a red corduroy skirt and a green jumper instead of my new school uniform, which made me feel immediately out of place when I arrived. In those days it was thought best to avoid emotional scenes. So, as soon as my trunk and bags had been taken into the junior school, my mother had a quick word with the matron and gave me a peck on the cheek.

'Well, goodbye darling – have a good term.' Then she turned on her heels and had gone before I had time to properly register our parting.

I was left to cope with the emotion alone. It was the pain of abandonment and the feelings of isolation that hurt so much. For the most part I allowed the tears to flow in private – in the bathroom or under the bedclothes, but it was not long before the pain inside reacted outwardly and I began suffering from excruciating earache. The matron was both severe in appearance and by nature. There was no hot-water-bottle, no drink, no advice, no word of sympathy.

'You can lie on your bed . . . for a little while.' And so I did and cried more.

Handicapped by age, a child is trapped by circumstance. The only freedom is to wander in the mind. No one could read my thoughts: they belonged to me. I yearned for the care that my mother had lavished on me when I had been sick at home. I longed for her love, I craved for a sense of family, and I bitterly regretted not having the courage to say what I needed to make me happy. But strength and weakness are oftentimes confused.

Why is it thought braver to stifle feelings rather than express them? Somehow it seems easier to bite one's tongue and suffer silently. If I complained I suspected that I would only be reprimanded and I did not have the courage to face that. So I decided that it was wiser not to seek comfort but to go it alone. Instead I began building walls of protection around myself as a way of minimising the impact of outside forces and repressing my more powerful emotions. How much simpler it seemed to block them off and begin to live a life of pretence. I imagined that the real me was safer hidden away within an imaginary box. But it did not take long before feelings of restriction began to emerge . . . a desire to break out.

I found it difficult to concentrate on my school work. I had neither the ability to achieve top grades easily, nor the vision to understand the value of mediocrity. I wanted more depth to my learning and the only subjects which offered that were Latin and English. Reading Virgil and conjuring up images of bee-keeping and Proteus riding the waves satisfied my escapist fantasies; whilst the occasional English essay enabled me to express my feelings in a way that would not damage my image of self-sufficiency.

I began an essay on Loneliness: 'To be alone and to be lonely are two quite different things . . . ' The teacher was pleased with me. No one else had made the distinction; but then I was familiar with the subject matter.

The world outside seemed temptingly normal. I pressed the day girls for information. 'What was for tea today? Did you take the dog out? Did you toast crumpets by the fire? I wish . . . '

I decided to break out. I wanted to go for a walk outside – at night. A friend who was similarly frustrated with school life decided to accompany me. We began to make plans. We were both in the same dormitory and there was a fire-escape which could be reached without detection from the bathroom next door. All we had to do was to scale across to it by way of a window-sill and drainpipe, and we calculated we could just about manage it. We went to bed in our clothes, hid our duffel coats under the bed and set the alarm for 1 am.

When we awoke we felt excited as the adrenaline began to flow. It was easier than we expected to get onto the fire-escape. We hurried down the iron steps, edged our way across the courtyard, then ran towards some trees and bushes knowing that we could use them for cover. We weaved our way across the lawns, through the orchard, and skirted round the boundary walls until we reached the wrought iron gates. They looked surprisingly forbidding at this time of night. We waited, watched, and when the coast seemed clear, we slipped out through the side entrance.

So we were out. We stood on the pavement and looked at each other. Where now? We had forged our way into the outside world but what were we going to do with the experience? We crossed the road and headed off towards the nearest shopping centre wondering what would be happening there at this time of night. It had started to drizzle and we quickened our step. When we got to the main street we peered round the corner. The street was empty. Not a soul in sight.

'Let's try this way.'

We walked on in silence keeping close to each other. Where was the entertainment? Did nothing go on at this time of night? I had never been out this late before. It did not take long before I began to feel vulnerable and alone out there at night in the middle of urban life – or no urban life. I wished there were some people about. After all, what we wanted was some fun and frivolity.

'What shall we do?' I asked tentatively.

'Let's go back.'

I was relieved though I tried not to show it. We turned around and saw in the distance a lone figure moving towards us.

'Is it the police? We're done for if it is.'

We altered our step to a confident stride to give the appearance of normality. After all, was there anything wrong with two fourteen-year-old girls being out in the middle of the night? The figure moved nearer and we moved faster. The rain had made the pavement slippery so we locked arms in case we fell. We knew that the gloom of the street lighting afforded us some protection as no one could see us unless they got up close. We reached the side road just as the figure stopped to take a good long look at us. Then we ran. We only paused for breath when we were inside the iron gates.

We stood there panting. We were back in school and yet I felt glad. It seemed the wrong way about and I did not understand why. Was the world outside really more scary than this ? Where did the answer to my dilemma lie? How was I to find a way out?

If there was no point in running away, then maybe I could escape into work. I had only just scraped through the last set of exams so I set myself the task of doubling my marks. I rose early to work in the library, studied late into the evening, and began to concentrate in lessons. It was a new experience. I enjoyed the self-imposed discipline of the routine and discovered a new-found confidence in knowing the answers in class. At the end of the summer our form was to be streamed into A and B groups – 'the swots and duds' – so there was the added incentive of my attaining A girl status. The exams came and my marks were equal to those of the brightest students.

'I would like to congratulate all those who attained an honours' average in their exams.'

My name was among the small number of girls who had achieved the top grade.

'Amazing. How did you do it?' My friends asked in surprise.

'I applied myself, I suppose.'

A week later the headmistress announced the form divisions. She read out the A group first. I waited expectantly . . . was it true? My name was not among them. I was choked as the realization hit home. My eyes filled up and I dropped my chin to my chest to conceal the tear that slithered down my cheek. I sat through the entire list until I heard my name resound out in the B group. I got up and marched out of the room.

'Well my dear,' my housemistress tried to console me later, 'we thought you would do better at the top of the bottom group than at the bottom of the top one.'

I remembered the race that I had run as a little girl when I was destined to end up the loser whichever way it went. So where were the rewards in life? I looked at the teacher's expressionless eyes and watched her empty gesturing in search of an answer. She had nothing to offer me. Her face was drawn, her gaze was vacant . . . no words she spoke could comfort me.

I wanted to leave. I never doubted that my parents wanted a good education for me. But what was a good education? I felt more trapped than liberated. In the holidays I was deprived of my friends, at school I was deprived of my family. The isolation left me feeling socially inept and inadequate. I had little political or social awareness, no knowledge of practical skills, no useful training that would equip me for the world, so all I could do was to fantasize about the future. Yes. It was time to unleash myself: I needed to experience a different kind of reality. At boarding-school I felt boarded up and the walls had to come down. My parents finally agreed that I could leave as soon as I was sixteen years old.

The day I left the air smelt fresh, the weather was clear and cumulus clouds studded the sky. Rain in the night had brightened up the green of the uncut grass and it smelt sweet and lush. I cast my eye across the lawns and noticed that the bushes were silvered by water droplets, then I glanced up at the monkey puzzle tree for the last time. Its height was impressive but I had always thought it looked strangely out of place by the school courtyard. Its maze of branches would confuse me no longer. I was off – out . . . away from there forever.

'Here, take this with you. It'll bring you luck.'

A friend stuck a sprig of shamrock in my lapel. 'It's Saint Patrick's day.'

Girls gathered around the car, crammed in the last of the bags, books and mementoes, and then in turn hugged me tight.

'Come on,' my mother chivvied, 'it's best that we go quickly.' She still did not like emotional scenes. To the waves and cheers of my friends, we sped off down the drive and out of the gates for the last time.

For years a group of girls had been thrown together – had struggled and strived for higher things, supported each other in

16

times of crisis and also shared in fun, mischief and games. Now it was time to go our separate ways. In just a moment all that intimacy was broken apart.

I was naïve but curious. I needed to experiment, make some mistakes, so that I could learn a little more about myself. I hugged my knees, sipped my tea and enjoyed the south-facing terrace. It was surrounded by sweet-smelling pink rose bushes. It seemed a shame that my father could never get rid of the mildew that tainted the flower heads. I let my eye wander across to the magnolia, then to the clematis that climbed up the almond tree, and on down to the two old pear trees that made a natural arch at the bottom of the garden. It felt good to be home. My father was back in Cambridge after seventeen years of working away, my mother was glad of my company since the rest of my siblings had left home, and I was relieved to have their undivided attention.

For the first time in my life I had a safe and solid base from which to play. Within a matter of weeks I had changed my life into a sketch book, and I allowed myself the time to create a myriad images in order that I could be drawn to those that attracted me most. I wanted to try everything, from prose to painting to sewing and designing. I ended up entering the world of make-believe, of painted scenery and made-up faces, of costumes and dance, of tricks and jokes. Increasingly I became absorbed in the theatre and before long landed myself with a part-time job in the Cambridge repertory.

I fell in love with the world of illusion – to me it felt more real than reality.

During time off my life was taken up with parties, pubbing and punting, for I had little responsibility except to arrive at the theatre on time to place the props, fix the lighting or help iron the costumes in the wardrobe department. My mind was opened to opera, drama and comedy, and 1965 was a good year for the Cambridge Footlights when talented folk were both treading the boards and writing skits and sketches.

'You got the only bad crit. David Frost said that our trousers weren't pressed properly. How about it eh?' And the performers laughed.

'Did he really say that?' I never knew when to believe them.

I laughed, I worked and fell in love. This time I scaled the walls, the college walls, and in the early hours of the morning, by the dim light of a small gas fire, experienced the delights of sex for the first time. It was gentle and full of tenderness – soothing caresses in the warm soft glow. I felt cherished and wanted. These were days of carefree abandon when restrictions were minimal and living and loving became synonymous with happiness and fun. An old borrowed Chevrolet would take us out into the countryside with beer, bread, cheese and doughnuts, to party on the fens, cool off in the river and return just in time for duty. We were able to be responsible without becoming too serious.

Life had transformed itself into an adventure, and now that I was discovering that there was fun in its play, I wanted to get more involved. Amidst the gaiety and games, I knew that I needed a direction if I were to move forward. I no longer felt oppressed by circumstance and I believed that I now had the confidence to take control. I had to find a path that suited me.

The theatre preoccupied me more than anything else, but I was never tempted to perform – it seemed difficult enough to understand oneself let alone become absorbed in other characters. The production and stage management aspects seemed more accessible – design, lighting, props., history of drama and costume, the holding together of a play so that it ran smoothly. No doubt it was because of my previous experience that I was offered a place at drama school – I was thrilled. I longed for a taste of student life and also looked forward to the move to London.

It was the cosmopolitan feel of the capital city that I liked. It seemed as though you could do anything, be anything, and not stand out from the crowd. Like a sequin stitched onto some glamourous ball gown, one could sparkle and yet disappear amid the thousand others that sparkled too. The sixties revolution generated a euphoria that instilled into us new excitement and energy. It was as though a sumptuous bowl of brightly coloured, luscious, tropical fruit oozing with juice had been placed before us on a table, and we were told to eat. And eat we did.

I was a sixties girl who led a sixties life – in moderation for the most part. But at times an inner voice cried out for something higher and more sublime, some resonance echoed in my soul. Within me, deep feelings were stirring that needed something more to satisfy them. My life in London began to be punctuated by visits to the opera with my father. It was here that his love of drama and music were combined to create the ultimate experience.

'The secret of Wagner is to let it wash over you.' My father winked at me and put his finger to his lips mischievously.

And for him life was mirrored through the great Wagnerian themes – of illusion and fantasy, of heroism and sacrifice, of love and death. He empathised with the passion of the Siegfrieds and Tristans, yet also understood the concerns and responsibilities of older men: to him there was a deeper meaning to the role of 'hero'. The power, pace and magnificence of the music fired his imagination and touched his soul and, when the great arias were sung, the poignant beauty of the human voice vibrated through his innermost being. I watched the tears flow down his cheeks.

For him music was a powerful love potion and, during that time, I was included in this love. I felt immensely privileged to share these moments. Under his guidance I was led forward gingerly. My horizons were expanded, my experience deepened, and I was given brief glimpses into another, more ephemeral world – one that I wanted to know more about.

By contrast, at college I immersed myself in the technical aspects of my course – the electrics, carpentry and sound engineering – and these were skills I could use anywhere. I enjoyed the challenge of wiring up the lights, fitting lanterns and splicing tapes, to achieve the right atmosphere on stage. At one moment I was painting flats for scenery, and the next 'breaking down' furniture to help it look worn and natural. I went from waving sheets of metal to simulate thunder, operating tabs and flies, even to managing a whole show.

Above all what mattered was to get on with the actors and win their trust. Their task was to pour their talent and energy into the character whether they were playing a bit part or taking a lead; the last thing that they wanted was to concern themselves with the technical aspects of a performance. The crew ran the play, and it was our duty to exude an air of efficiency and infallibility to instil confidence in the performers. I enjoyed most of the jobs and had no particular preference whether I was assigned the task of stage manager or technician, indeed it was the variety of work that I found stimulating.

'You'll be on electrics for The Doll's House.'

This meant that after the lighting arrangements had been set up, I remained on a six-foot-high platform lowering and raising levers on cue. It was a strange kind of responsibility to have control over all those pools of light on stage. Although they had been carefully designed to blend with each other, from my position I was completely oblivious to the illusion that was being created. All I had in front of me was a row of controls.

No doubt it was easy to make mistakes. It was simply a question of moving the right lever at the wrong time or the wrong lever at the right time, and the lighting designer's plans would be drastically upset and the actors thrown into a state of confusion. And so it was that when Doctor Rank made his final entrance stage left, my concentration lapsed momentarily and, when the spotlight to highlight him was supposed to come up, another spot went down and the stage was plunged into darkness. I never realized what had happened, though suddenly it went very quiet on stage.

A resonant voice called up to me. 'May I have some light on my entrance please?'

And that was how I met Martin. He was in the last year of his acting course at the Central School, and the stage management students learned their trade by working on the actors' plays. It was to these final productions that directors and agents came to spot new talent that would soon be treading the professional boards. At the end of the show it was down to the local pub to celebrate a good performance or drown a bad one.

'It's good to make mistakes – you learn from them.' Martin reassured me on the lighting fiasco.

'I'm sorry about that. You can't see what's going on from up there.'

'Are you planning to be a stage manager?'

'No, I think I'd like to work in television, possibly directing.' I wanted to impress. 'What about you?'

'Henry V and Hamlet.'

'Set your sights high don't you?'

'No point in going into this profession unless you do.'

'Have you ever thought of doing anything else?'

'Yes . . . I was going to be a doctor.'

'That's quite a switch!' I turned to mingle with my fellow students.

College days were about sharing ideas, dreams and pints of beer at The Winchester, or 'Winch.' as we used to call it. It was certainly true that I wanted to go into television, but to direct? I was a long way off from that. But aspirations, even if fantastical, kept us focused while we worked on our theatre projects. Student days gave us all the chance to imagine ourselves in different careers. Reality would bump home soon enough.

'I like the wildness of the moors – sheep and stone walls.' Martin was leaning over my shoulder and whispering in my ear. He had found me again in the crush.

I was intrigued. 'I do too. There's a sense of freedom once you get into the open.'

'In Yorkshire there are some remote places. Once you get out onto the tops you can see for miles and there's only the hardy sheep to keep you company. But it's dangerous to be out there alone when the mists come down.'

'I've spent quite a lot of time in Cornwall over the years. I love the sense of space. Ever fancied being a shepherd?' I asked impishly.

'I'd probably enjoy it. I like being out in all weathers feeling the sun, wind and rain on my face. Are you coming with me? I mean, back to my place.' He was straight-forward and I liked that.

In the fusty smelling world of bed-sit land, floral wallpaper and candlewick counterpanes were the norm. Coffee was drunk as a prelude, an excuse for waiting a little . . . I was intrigued by this man who seemed to penetrate my veils of illusion. He held my head firmly in his hands and turned me towards him. 'You know something? I believe you want to be wanted.'

Was he astute or just full of guile? I realized that I was an idealist and a romantic, but at last I felt that I was being offered some understanding by someone, even though I had only just met him. I looked into his eyes searching for answers and then put my hand up to his face to touch . . . to see that he was real. He drew me to him and I held on tight. Throughout my life I had been looking for love – I had wanted it so much. I could not bear this moment to disappear in a whirl of dreams.

To a girl of eighteen, love unexpectedly appeared in the form of a hauntingly good-looking youth with classic features and penetrating green eyes, who swept me off my feet and told me I was his. Passion numbs the mind and quietens reason and, as the powerful waves of emotion engulfed me, maybe it was obvious that I would leave myself open and vulnerable. Who can predict how a young woman will respond to those powerful emotions of love and desire? Logic is defied. To me, all that mattered was that those feelings went on and on and on . . . and my actions became orchestrated to that cause alone. After all, that is what I had long been searching for – the feeling of being loved and wanted. With that goal alone in mind, it is easy to be thrown off course.

Life has strange twists that help to make up its rich tapestry. The ingredients of this tale are a week in Cornwall, youthful passion, a fecund teenager, Easter time, barbers' shops that were closed for the holiday, and a time when supplies of contraceptives were limited. The result was inevitable. One night temptation lured us on too far . . . and Rachel was conceived.

Some may surmise that turmoil would ensue, but that was not the case for me. One false negative test postponed confirmation of my state until I was almost three months pregnant. Student friends were growing sinisterly accustomed to the abortion clinics at a time when contraceptive help for single women was scarce. Even the doctor seemed surprised when I said I wanted to have the child. I assured him that I was delighted at the thought of having a baby to care for and bring up. He was an elderly man with a kind wrinkled face: he looked at me quizzically, smiled and said, 'Good luck to you lass!'

I went to Cambridge to tell my parents. They regarded it their duty to remind me of alternatives.

'You could have the child adopted you know.'

'I don't want to have the child adopted.'

'Think of the ties at your age. You can't even go to the corner shop alone.'

'I know that.'

'There's no recrimination on our part – we want you to understand that.'

And I knew there was not. My parents offered me their sympathy and support, but they could see that their younger daughter was relinquishing her career and independence for a life of nappies, baby cries and parental responsibilities.

'But you haven't lived . . . ' They tried to warn me.

'I'm about to start.'

'Where will you stay. What will you do?'

'We'll get married. There are a couple of theatre agents who want to take Martin on. We'll be alright . . . really we will.'

There is a refreshing innocence and optimism when young, an ability to live in the present and not cower before the future. Life experience makes us more cautious as we grow older. Influenced by past successes, we fear failure and its subsequent repercussions and so begin to tread more gingerly, missing out on the drama and the razzmatazz. I wanted to live close to the edge. It was there that the unpredictable lay in wait, unseen, like a wild cat ready to pounce. The idea of the humdrum frightened me. It seemed that one had the prospect of either allowing oneself to be carried along by life's turbulent stream, accepting all the inherent dangers, or remaining in a pool that might grow stagnant in time.

I wanted flow and tumbling waterfalls.

The wedding was a discreet affair that took place on a Saturday in Cambridge to ensure that neither of us would miss college; and a night away at my godmother's country house persuaded us that we had not been cheated of a honeymoon. My prize possession was a second-hand car and, although our intention was to teach Martin to drive as soon as possible, that responsibility was at present left to me. It was while I was negotiating the country lanes as we drove back to London that Martin revealed a strange side of his character: he suddenly began to taunt me. For no apparent reason he began throwing money out of the car window. His action frightened me. Not only was I totally unprepared for such unexpected behaviour, but I was also alarmed at the prospect of losing our meagre resources. As soon as I stopped the car I realized the futility of searching for coins among the hedgerows but, each time I drove on, more were thrown. I could find no way out of my predicament: I was trapped. However, just as unexpectedly as this bizarre performance had started, it ceased. Nevertheless the scenario made me nervous and I found it difficult to concentrate on the traffic as we approached the metropolis. My mind was dwelling on our future. I had made my choice and all I could do was to try and make it work.

My tutors were sorry to see me finish my course prematurely, especially when it was only going to be replaced with house-hunting and baby-care tasks. But, within these challenges, I was soon to have my first taste of reality when I discovered how difficult it was to find a landlord who would trust a young couple to be responsible. I could hardly blame them. We scoured London for somewhere to live only to be greeted by lame excuses, ludicrously high rents, doors shut in our faces and filthy properties. Only a month before I was due to have the baby, we were forced to look for a place just south of London. There at last we met a wealthy, sympathetic landowner who owned two manor houses.

'I've got an estate cottage that's been renovated but there's no road to it yet – it's across a field.'

'It doesn't matter – really. Please can we take it? Can we have it now?' We were desperate.

'You want me to say yes, don't you?' He said looking down at my stomach. 'But how will you manage the rent? Actors are renowned for 'resting' every now and again.' And then, as if struck by a thought, he added. 'I'll tell you what, you can do a bit of decorating for me when you need some extra money. How about it?'

That suited us very well. Friends and family carried our few bits of furniture and belongings across the field and we had a home . . . at least for a while.

Remote places and mud tracks became an integral part of my life for the next couple of years. Martin quickly passed his driving test and I realized that the struggles that beset a newly fledged actor were to become my struggles too. I soon came to the conclusion that our lives would never be settled. After Rachel was born it became three of us that had to move with the work, wherever that was, if we were to stay together.

As we travelled to Pitlochry with the old mini piled high with baby gear and necessities for a year, it seemed a long way away from friends, family and familiarity. We drove through the night. At the end of the following day we reached a cottage with a red corrugated-iron roof, that was set against the hillside at the end of a long, rough track with three gates. We were greeted by a damp musty smell and decoration that appeared to be from another age. There was no electricity either. The water was heated by a fire that someone had lit in readiness for our arrival. Drop scones had been left out on the table for tea.

I reacted uncontrollably by crying out. 'I can't stay here. I won't. Ten months in a place like this and I'll go mad.'

'It's alright.' Martin reassured me patiently. 'We'll find somewhere else in the village where you'll have some people nearby. We'll ask around in the morning.'

'Promise?'

'I promise. There must be other places for rent I suppose.'

Rachel looked up from her Moses basket. She was the only one that was smiling – a bonny, well-behaved three-month-old babe.

But we never bothered to move: it seemed too much of an upheaval since we were only there for nine months. Instead I took up the challenge of making it work. On an income of twelve pounds a week, I managed to pay the rent, buy essential provisions, get a bottle of gas for the stove, and just have enough left over for our weekly pint and a half of beer at the local pub. I kept myself occupied by looking after Rachel and going for walks. Meanwhile Martin rehearsed during the day and performed at night. When at home he was caring and supportive for the most part; but just occasionally feelings of frustration would explode in a display of temper that took me by surprise and left me feeling vulnerable and scared. I was not used to being at the receiving end of such powerful and erratic emotions. But it was the evenings alone that I found interminably long, stuck out there in the middle of nowhere with only the sound of the wind whipping around the window panes and the transistor radio for company. Sometimes it felt eerie. I learned to knit to keep my hands busy. And, when it got late and Martin had still not returned, I would gently lift Rachel out of her cot and take her into bed with me for comfort.

It was a time of drawing in, a time in which I had to learn to readjust to a different kind of reality . . . one that had echoes of my time at school. I had deliberately turned my back on a vibrant and colourful world full of possibility, and replaced it with one of self-imposed limitation. Why? I asked myself. Was this living close to the edge?

I had cast myself to the winds, or so it seemed. Occasionally their power seemed so strong that I was afraid. At times I found strength from facing them, other times I would curl up and cower my head as a way of protecting myself. How much choice did I have? Was I being drawn along by a much greater force that I could not defy, or did I have the means to cut the strings and take control myself? I did not know . . .

2

I wheeled and bumped the pram across the neighbouring fields, along farm tracks and then up into forest where the tall Scots pine grew. There the trees had been thinned to allow enough light and space for natural regeneration to take place. This allowed the older trees to reach full height and they towered above me showing off their majesty and strength. I stared up at the canopy, craning my neck back until I became dazzled by the patterns of sunlight spilling through the branches, then looked down to watch the insects foraging among the mulch on the forest floor. Small, tender saplings struggled up to reach the light. The place inspired me. It was cathedral-like, quiet and sublime.

I wanted change. I wanted to lift myself out of Scottish mists and move to a place where I could listen to a less melodious tune. I was still young – I needed pace. I had had enough of mud tracks and remoteness and was no longer prepared to keep up the pretence of life being a romantic adventure. How easy it was to be deluded. I knew that in order to change my own circumstances, it meant that Martin had to change his. Our lives were inextricably linked. ·

'Let's go back to London,' I suggested positively.

'I have to go where the work is – you know that.'

'A large town then . . . most theatres are in towns except for this one.'

'I can't just conjure up work where you want it.'

'Why not?' I asked innocently and smiled. 'We'll try together.'

So try we did. We both immersed ourselves in the task of

finding out about repertory theatres, forthcoming productions, the right people to contact and – having resurrected my old portable typewriter – we then began writing scores of letters to theatres, directors and casting agents. We worked well together. No stone was left unturned, no potential acting part excluded and, when our task was accomplished, we waited hopefully for the replies to come in.

'*Thank you for your letter but I am afraid* . . . ' But we never felt deterred by rejection, so buoyed up were we by the conviction that we would succeed. Each refusal just fired us up with fresh determination to try again. We only needed one expression of interest, just one director to make the connection between an acting role and Martin. And, as time went by, we became more and more convinced that good, prestigious work was just around the corner.

'Oh for pavements and some city life!' I shouted as we skidded off through the mud. 'I'm not going back to that Kent field for long.'

The rain refreshed us as we opened and shut the gates of the farm track for the last time. The season had come to an end.

'A flat in London would be nice,' Martin mused.

'Audition first, job second and then a flat. Right Rachel?'

'Da - da . . ' she quacked from the back of the car. She was almost one year old.

Convinced that success was imminent, we never doubted that Martin would perform well in his audition at the Hampstead Theatre Club, and that he would be offered the part of the juvenile lead in the A. A. Milne play. We realized that this would not only give him the chance of being seen in London, but would also provide him with the opportunity of showing that he could be trusted with a major role. It seemed like a new beginning for us both. In the following weeks the critics heralded promising new talent and our confidence grew. One play led to another, and it was not long before our income became steady enough to allow us to move into a top floor flat in Maida Vale.

'You need some new photographs, Martin.' His new agent was

keen and astute. 'Go and see John Vere Brown. He specializes in taking pictures of actors.'

It transpired that John would have much preferred to work with oils and canvas than with a camera, but photography earned him his living. When he captured a person on film, it was an impression, a glance that he caught, which seemed to pull the viewer deep into the picture. It was as though he had the ability to reveal the thoughts in a person's mind. His pictures made one sit up and take note. But it was the sense of mystery that was intriguing about the photographs he took of Martin. His eyes had depth and intensity, while his expression contained a remoteness, a softness, that was strangely alluring. It made one want to know more.

Federico Fellini, film director extraordinaire, did want to know more. For Fellini the right look, the right face were crucial. At the time he was looking across Britain and America for someone of Anglo-Saxon origin to play the lead in his next film, Satyricon, which was set in pre-Christian Rome. When the photographs of Martin landed on the director's desk, the face seemed to fit and Fellini asked to meet the young actor. Then he asked for more photographs, and screen tests, followed by more tests alongside contenders for other roles; and finally there was lunch at a prestigious Chinese restaurant in London. It was apparent that Fellini wanted to discover as much as possible about Martin. Could he really become his latest protégé?

When we finally heard that Martin had been offered the part of Encolpius, we were astonished, delighted and over-awed. Neither of us could believe his success. It seemed incredible that such momentous change could happen so quickly. Corks popped, the champagne flowed, and excited telephone calls were made to the rest of the family so that everyone could share in the celebrations. A nine-month film contract was signed, and we were off to Rome . . . or so I thought.

I was dusting when I heard Martin on the stairs. His footsteps sounded heavier, more ponderous than usual. I paused to shake the duster out of the bedroom window then turned and looked at him. He seemed nervous.

'I need to talk to you.'

I sensed an unease. 'Yes . . . what about?'

'I've been thinking . . . '

'Yes?' I wanted him to get on with it.

'Just to say . . . do you realize that this is my first proper film part?'

'Of course I realize.'

'It's very important to me. A lot depends on it – my future for a start.' He laughed awkwardly and then suddenly grew serious. 'I've just got to be able to concentrate, do you understand?'

'So?' I was beginning to feel distinctly uncomfortable.

'So I don't want you to come.' He spoke hurriedly.

'Come? What do you mean? Come where?'

'I don't want you to come to Italy.'

'What?' There was a grating edge to my voice as I spoke.

'It's my first film, you must understand that . . . it's very important. I need to go and do it alone.'

'But you can't leave me here. What will I do? What about Rachel?' I wanted to remain calm, but I knew I could feel myself beginning to tremble.

'I know it's difficult for you, believe me . . . I realize that. But I can't go and play this part with a young wife and child hanging around my neck.'

His words stung.

'You can't do this to us Martin. We've worked for this together. I mean, Rachel and I . . . we won't get in the way I promise . . . really we won't.' I could hear the air of desperation in my voice as it got more shrill. 'I just want to be there with you. Please, please. I don't want to stay here by myself.'

'Eliza, you're not coming. I've made up my mind and that's that.' He turned briskly and left the room.

Dazed, I fell back on the bed, cradling my head in my arms. Rocking to and fro I murmured softly to myself, 'No, no . . . please no . . . please, please no. I can't – I can't bear it. No . . . NO.'

I sat up abruptly. Couldn't he hear me? Of course he could. I stared at the door sternly, angrily. How on earth could he do this to me? How could he land me in this impossible position?

Then suddenly, out of the corner of my eye, I caught a movement at the window.

I gasped under my breath. 'Oh my God . . . '

We were four floors up and Rachel was crawling out of the window. At first I found it difficult to register what was happening. Maybe it was only moments, but it seemed as though minutes passed before I could gather my thoughts together and readjust to the new scenario. There Eliza – just over there – your daughter is perched on the sill, half-way out of a top floor window looking at the traffic in the street. Of course. I must have left it open after shaking the duster.

Quickly and quietly, I dropped to the floor reckoning that any sound or movement could startle her. Then gingerly I edged my way towards her, remembering my stalking skills when I had played on the Cornish cliffs as a child. I kept my head low down, aware that she remained still while she was burbling away to herself. If prayers were answered according to the intensity of passion with which they were offered, I need not have worried. From some elusive and unfathomable place deep inside me, I pleaded with a God somewhere – anywhere – NOT to let my child fall. I got closer. Still she was aware neither of her imminent danger, nor of her potential rescuer behind. I knew that it was going to be difficult to judge when I was near enough to reach out and grab her without startling her into fright. Her little feet were just inside the room. Could I get them from here? I thought so. Yes. Boldly I went for her.

I took her in my arms, held her tight and let my tears flow over her. I loved her so, so much.

To live one's hopes and dreams through a partner is a precarious thing to do. Occasionally a hard kick is needed. Wake up! Find your own path. But it is difficult to wrench apart two lives that have become so closely intertwined. How could I begin to disentangle them? My world had become painted with a wash of grey and, though I wanted some colour to cheer myself up, I did not know how to find it.

The sinus headaches started as soon as Martin left for Italy. Each step I took, searing pain cut through my head like a knife to the point when it became impossible for me to look after Rachel by myself. I had no choice but to take refuge with my parents until I was better. It was time out, time to readjust. When I returned to London I felt stronger and more able to cope with my new-found predicament.

It felt as though a curtain had been dropped across my path and, although I made attempts to tear it down, each time I did I just became more aware of its presence. I had lost touch with my college friends, turned my back on my career, I was restricted by a small child, I had no prospects, no real interests either . . . except, of course, for Martin. My twenty-first birthday came and went . . . alone – the only consolation being some trinkets that arrived in a packet from Rome.

It was not until the middle of December that Martin telephoned.

'We've got a two-week break over Christmas. Why don't you and Rachel come over? We can go up to the mountains for a holiday, find a little place to stay. If you come a bit early you can see some filming on the set. How about it?'

'Yes – oh yes.' I was filled with excitement and anticipation.

Where does reality end and illusion begin? With Fellini it was impossible to say where any boundaries lay. He was absorbed in a world of his own making and the characters he created walked on a knife-edge wondering to which world they belonged. He encouraged the actor to merge with the role, for any sharp dividing lines to blur. Martin and Encolpius . . . to Fellini they were one, just as different aspects of a person combine to form one character. Encolpius the adventurer, the lover of both men and women, the handsome blue-eyed youth who was not afraid of immersing himself in life's drama and experiencing its extremes. And Encolpius the poet and philosopher, who realized how easy it is for humankind to get swallowed up by lust and greed in the endless search for more. Encolpius was both the consumer and observer of life.

The world of make-believe lures us into realms where the imagination can fly free. Here we can break out of boundaries. To be released momentarily from rules, dogma and convention, allows fantasy to take over, a thought to be extended beyond its norm. We are taken beyond self-imposed limitations. Stories and legends, characters and costumes, allow the distant lands of our mind to be brought up close – sometimes poetically, sometimes terrifyingly. Through writers and artists we are reminded that these lands exist.

Rome buzzed. The raised emotions and voices, the honking of horns, the chaotic elegance that prevailed throughout the capital city engulfed me as soon as I arrived.

Martin seemed pleased to see his family again. 'We'll eat at Ceserina's restaurant tonight. She claims to do the finest selection of pasta in Italy. Hiram will join us – you'll like him.'

Hiram was an American actor who was playing the part of Encolpius's rebellious young friend. I looked forward to meeting him.

'You must come to Cinecitta tomorrow and watch us film.' Hiram encouraged me across the dining table.

'Which part are you doing?'

'The Garden of the Suicides – it will be a beautiful scene to watch.'

'Will it?' I sounded surprised.

'Yes, I think so. It will be moving.' Hiram paused and looked down at his plate. 'You've got to remember that this film takes place at a time when all morality had broken down and decadence had become the way of life. Heads rolled for no other reason than a little bit of envy or greed. Limbs were chopped off for entertainment. And everyone was consumed by an insatiable appetite for sex, food or both. I've never seen so many obese unclothed men and women before – Fellini's macabre circus of characters. Many of them are so odd, you wonder where he dreams them up from. No, The Suicides will be a far more sensitive scene – and the leading characters are a talented couple.' He smiled. 'You'll be intrigued, you'll see.'

Ceserina interrupted Hiram's flow to check that the food was up to standard.

'*Ciao*! How are you tonight *mi bambini*? Ah, you have your wife here Martino . . . *bello*. How long are you here for?'

'Until after Christmas.'

'Enjoy yourself – enjoy Roma. It's a place you take into your heart – live it, breathe it and love it – that's what you have to do.' And she spread her arms wide as if to absorb the whole city.

'I'll do my best. The pasta is . . . *magnifico*.' I enthused, and it was true.

'*Va bene.*'

The car arrived early the next morning. It was the usual routine for Martin: a five o'clock start, the drive to the film studios, a session of weight training to build up his biceps, then into hair and make-up for an hour's meticulous grooming, and at last breakfast. I was surprised how long it took.

'It's as though I've done a morning's work before filming has even begun.'

We wandered down to the studio and I looked around, amazed by the vastness of the place. There were numerous sets that corresponded to different scenes in the film, each one as big as a theatre, and some that reached so high they disappeared from view altogether.

'Will the whole film be shot here?' I asked Hiram.

'Most of it – apart from the sea scenes.'

'It's extraordinary – it seems so real. A different time recaptured in a large shed.'

'It's more incredible to watch Fellini film. Notice how he uses the camera.'

The scene was a simple courtyard with an elegant stool placed in the middle of it. One or two frescoes decorated the walls and a line of tall silvery bushes offered shade to the villa at one side. Peacocks strutted about while some children played with an iron hoop in the foreground. The owners of the villa were a young noble couple, whose lands and belongings were wanted by

Caesar who was claiming estates indiscriminately. They knew that the soldiers would be coming soon. They summoned their servants who lined up before them.

Their master offered a libation and then spoke quietly: 'My will is that this man, this youth, and this . . . ' His voice faltered. 'All of you are free.'

He anointed each of them individually.

'Thank you master, thank you.' The women looked gratefully into his eyes, an old man hugged his master.

He tried to console them. 'Tomorrow the soldiers will come and confiscate our lands, but they won't find us here. Do not be concerned.'

Then the freed slaves loaded their belongings onto a wooden cart and left. It was the turn of the children next. The three daughters and two sons stood in front of their parents and waited. Suddenly the youngest girl, who had a head of fair curls, ran forward.

'Will you come tomorrow?'

Her father knelt down and took her in his arms and held her tight.

She whispered in his ear. 'Papa, where we are going may be beautiful, but I won't believe it unless you say it. Is it beautiful?'

'Yes.' He looked across at the others. Their eyes met. His eldest son walked forward and offered his head for blessing. His father ran his fingers through his hair. Their mother embraced each one of them in turn. Slowly the children moved away towards the second cart that had been made ready for them. They climbed up onto it and, as it pulled away, they waved good-bye.

The master sat on the stool, let out a short nervous laugh, and then took a knife from inside his robe. He slit his wrists firmly and accurately. His wife came out of the villa carrying some wine, berries and a small brazier with some fire burning in it. She noticed that her husband's wrists were flowing with blood. He looked across at her. 'You're pale. Pour us some wine.'

She knelt down beside him.

His voice was getting fainter. 'Don't do it. I know you will . . . but you mustn't.'

She offered him some wine and took some for herself. Then she watched him while remaining quite still. After a while he became too weak to hold himself upright any more. He slumped over onto the stool. She then placed some poisonous berries in her wine and drank.

Ascyltus appeared from behind the line of bushes, looked across the courtyard, and beckoned to his friend Encolpius. They seemed apprehensive, cautious. Encolpius put his arm around his friend protectively. In front of them lay the two dead bodies of the master and mistress.

Fellini's art and expertise was to capture the story on celluloid. 'Now zoom in tight on their faces – closer still – each one in turn. Right. Then very slowly take the camera round – like this.' Briefly Fellini took charge of the camera. He was filming the children's expressions. I listened to Fellini's soft mesmeric voice while the scene was being shot, talking first to the cameraman and then to the children. I looked across at the line of faces. Little seemed to be happening. I wondered where the action was taking place.

'Watch closely,' Hiram whispered in my ear. 'Fellini can even reveal the thoughts in their heads. Look again. That flicker of an eyelid, a hint of a smile, the look in their faces. So much is happening . . . and the camera is picking it all up.'

'Run it again.' Fellini instructed.

I edged a little closer, and this time followed the line of the camera round more carefully. As it lingered on each face I could see Fellini looking intently at each child, gently coaxing from them the right expression so that they radiated the feeling that he wanted. It was as though he was willing it to be right. Youth, innocence, a long lost look with deep sad eyes . . . yes, I was beginning to understand what Fellini was trying to do. And he was achieving it. His direction was masterful and I felt moved as I watched him work.

'You see?'

'Yes I do.'

And, fleetingly, I imagined myself to be a photographer.

On the drive home when we reached the outskirts of the city I noticed fires burning at the side of the road. 'What are they for?' I asked Martin.

'Prostitutes. They sit beside them and tempt men on their way back from work. The high-class girls work in the centre, places like the Via Veneto.'

'What are they like . . . the high-class ones?'

'How would I know?'

I glanced across at him and smiled. 'No, of course you wouldn't.'

Straight after Christmas Martin, Rachel and I left for Spoleto and the mountains. A high village, a small *albergo*, a comfortable room for the three of us, and it felt as though we were hidden away in the middle of nowhere. Each day we would walk along the narrow mountain tracks, taking with us some cold chicken, bread, cheese and a bottle of wine. Snow lay on the ground, the air smelt clean and fresh and we breathed it in deep to rid ourselves of city grime. It made a sharp contrast to the traffic-choked streets of Rome. We could discern a few broken down walls trailing off into the distance between the hills; they seemed to have little relevance now. But, as we walked on to the remoter valleys, we came across shepherds' huts made of rough-hewn stone that we presumed were used as refuges for summer feeding pastures. We knew that we were far away from home.

As we picnicked, we basked in the warmth of the winter sun and talked.

'Is it difficult working for Fellini?' I wanted to find out more about Martin's life in Rome.

'No, he's been very kind – rather like a father figure. One day I was so exhausted I felt I couldn't go on. I broke down and cried. But he just came over and put his arm round me and said, "Now, Martino, everything is alright – *non importante* – nothing matters you know. You go out and enjoy yourself tonight." It's demanding having to be there on set every day, all made-up ready to perform, whether you're needed or not. It's been three months solid now.'

'I can see that.' I had witnessed at first hand the pressure he was under.

'But there's more to it than that.'

'What do you mean?'

'Fellini keeps on encouraging me to experiment . . . to be free.'

'In what way?'

'I'm supposed to be an Encolpius – someone who takes risks.'

'Risks?' I was confused.

'Eliza, I want you to understand.' There was a sense of urgency in Martin's voice. 'I am playing a part which Fellini believes should take over my life. On the one hand, he's telling me to come out of my shell and party, have women, live life and so on, and on the other hand I have you and Rachel waiting in England for me to come home. I feel as though I'm being pulled in two, work on one side and family on the other. I hardly know what I should be doing any more. You know how much I care for you both, don't you?'

I waited for a little while before responding. I was aware of how easy it is for words to come out wrong, for their meaning to be misinterpreted.

'When we married we were very young. I never wanted us to feel trapped. I suppose I knew that you were bound to roam a bit . . . ' I paused to gather my thoughts. I sensed that he was being unfaithful to me but I did not want to react childishly . . . though I was hardly more than a child myself. 'But I always want to know what's happening between us. I don't want to be kept in the dark. I don't like secrets because then suspicion, deceit, lies, all those things build up. I won't feel so hurt about what you do if you tell me what's going on.' I spoke firmly so as to reinforce the meaning.

I wanted my words to be true. Indeed I expressed a sentiment that was to become a navigational guide that would steady us throughout our relationship. At that moment, high on that Appenine hillside, I felt that openness and talking together meant more to me than the temporary pain I might feel from his wanderings – a fling with some pretty Italian girl or a high class tart, the experience of some new drug or a brief homosexual encounter. His telling me about it seemed to bring me closer to him. I felt more included and the hurt was neutralized.

Martin sat back and took Rachel onto his knee for comfort and warmth. She had walked a long way for her young age.

'In the film Eumolpius the old poet says when he's dying: "I can only leave you poetry – the wind, the sun, the sea, the good earth and the mountains, the streams, the clouds that pass by. You will look at them and remember our brief friendship."' Martin glanced across at me, and then looked up at the sky before continuing with his story. 'Eumolpius lies back and looks at the star-studded heavens and says: "I love you Love. These stars are like the tears of Love . . . I leave you all this, all of this."' And Martin cast his arm around the skies.

We both fell silent. Martin spoke first. 'Eumolpius isn't bothered about what happens to him, what he has or doesn't have . . .'

'I bet he is.'

'You're probably right. For all his fine words he's a bit of a hypocrite. Maybe that's why I like him. At one point he's saying how lust for money causes decadence and that man's ideal should be Virtue, and the next he's amassing his own fortunes. He dies before he can enjoy them anyway.'

'What happens to you?'

'Ascyltus dies . . . he's stabbed by a boatman. And Encolpius goes off for more adventures. What a guy! He finds a ship that's sailing for Africa and joins the crew. The winds are favourable, the clouds are breaking up and . . . ' Martin looked across at the distant line of hills and spoke softly, enunciating each word. '"We visited unknown cities. For the first time I heard the names of Kelisha, Rectis. On an island covered with high perfumed grass, a young Greek told us that in the years . . ." and then it suddenly ends. The frame freezes with Encolpius sailing off into the sunset.'

I smiled at the picture in my mind.

'Talking of which, maybe we should be heading back?'

Rachel had been chewing on a piece of bread. 'Ready, I'm ready,' she said, pleased at the prospect of moving. Martin picked her up and put her on his shoulders while I packed up the food. We set off fast along the track before night closed in.

It was planned that as soon as Martin started filming again, Rachel and I would fly back to England. So, early in January, we left the winter sun of Italy and the bright lights of Rome and arrived back in London on a grey, wintry day.

The following months passed more quickly. Inspired by what I had seen in Rome, I bought a camera and began taking portraits of Rachel. I learned about darkroom techniques and even bought a few chemicals. The weather was getting warmer which meant that I could go out for longer pavement walks. I also befriended a thirteen-year-old Indian girl called Bhanu. She lived with her many brothers and sisters directly across the road and, when released from home and school duties, she liked to spend time playing with Rachel.

'Eliza,' she would run up the stairs and say, 'can I take Rachel please?'

'Willingly,' I agreed readily. I relished the idea of having some time to myself. Bhanu would then sweep Rachel up in her arms and disappear over the road. An hour or two later she would bring her back smelling of spices and with her hair covered with oil. 'It makes it grow,' she assured me. Other times Bhanu would spend the afternoon at our house trying to explain in her broken English how to cook special Gujurati recipes.

It was to this relatively simple lifestyle that Martin eventually returned in the early summer. By then he had been away for almost ten months.

It had been arranged that the film première was to be held at the Venice Film Festival. I became concerned over what I should wear. I had no celebrity or film star status. All I had to do was to appear as Martin's wife, so I thought it would be inappropriate to dress too glamorously; it was not my style anyway. I went from shop to shop searching the hanging rails, until I found a simple white Mexican cotton dress that I did not like very much, but it seemed to suit my feelings of vulnerability.

We flew direct to Venice where special motor boats had been arranged to take us to the Lido and our hotels. Fellini had arrived with his wife and the other stars, and the paparazzi were out in force.

'Who are you?' I was asked.

'Martin's wife.'

'You go in that boat then.'

Martin was taken off to be photographed, while I was sent along to the end boat on the quay. It was a surprise to be split up so early in the trip. I did not see Martin or the other actors again until we arrived at the hotel. After a few courtesies we were taken to our room. As we were shown in by the porter, I must have looked shocked. Anxiously he asked me if everything was alright.

'Oh yes . . . it's just so big.'

It seemed completely out of proportion to anything that I had imagined. We had clearly been allocated one of the grandest rooms in the hotel and I felt over-awed by it. It accentuated my feelings of naïvety and lack of experience.

It had been arranged that the actors would take part in a parade on the way to the cinema. We would then watch the screening of the film and afterwards the stars would appear on stage to receive the audience's applause. We washed and dressed in readiness for the occasion and, in a way that was completely out of character for me, I painted on layers of dark eye make-up and twisted my hair up on top of my head. I was nervous and maybe thought that this was a way I could hide. But that would have been difficult. We gathered in the hotel lobby, stars to the front and appendages to the rear, and proceeded to walk to the cinema, elbowing our way through the crowds and the cameras. Martin was aware of my feelings of intimidation, but he was nervous himself and could do little to support me as he had to be out in front promoting himself. Smiles, show, glitz and glamour, and the interminable clicks – it was all there. Surely people would be wondering who on earth I was.

I felt small and insignificant . . . a nobody amidst those who believed they were somebody.

At one point Fellini caught my eye. 'So Eliza, what do you think?'

What did I think? What did he think of me, I wondered to myself. I quickly averted my gaze and muttered something indistinguishable under my breath. When would this interminable nightmare end?

I wanted to see the film in London amongst ordinary people who would laugh, sneer, be shocked, jolted out of their everyday existence. I would be able to concentrate there, to enjoy the performances and the camera work. I wanted to be amongst objective critics. Here in Venice, it was not the right time. The predominantly Italian audience was bound to be impressed by their director's work and, as the film rolled, they clearly were. At last the final frame. Encolpius had gone off into the sunset. As soon as the credits had finished I had no choice but to follow Fellini and his entourage backstage. I had nowhere else to go. Someone raised a hand to stop me going on stage. I felt like screaming at him: 'Don't worry, I know my place.'

Instead I waited patiently in the wings while the applause went on and on. I wanted this crazy world of dreams to end. I wanted to go home.

When someone discovers that they are out of their depth and cannot swim, they reach out wildly in search of any solid structure that they can grab on to. When they find it, they cling on so tight that the blood drains from their veins and their knuckles go white. How often had I felt as though I was gasping for air . . . in need of some aid to hold myself up. Somehow I had to take some control over my life, instead of feeling that I was being controlled by it.

As a child I had heard myself described as independent and strong-willed. I knew that this was largely an act put on to impress others. This outer performance was just a way of concealing my deep feelings of vulnerability. But if I had the strength to hide my feelings so convincingly, then surely I had the will-power to take charge of my own destiny. I could no longer afford to be a victim of outside forces. Yes – there lay the answer.

When I was a child I had found comfort in the idea of escape. Now I wanted control . . . control over myself.

One morning I decided to have only one slice of toast instead of two. My mother's home-made marmalade was tempting and when it was spread on hot-buttered toast, the tastes and textures melded wonderfully. I was often tempted to eat more than I intended.

'I think I'll be more careful about what I eat,' I said to Martin as if to enforce my decision.

'Why?'

'I have to compete with those actress friends of yours!' I laughed to conceal my embarrassment.

'But you look fine.'

'That's not the point.'

'Well what is the point?'

'I'm not sure.'

The weeks drew into months, as one film or play led to the next, one trip to another, from touring England to Denmark to the Island of Bali and then back to London again. I joined Martin when he thought it was appropriate, but I knew that I had to establish a greater sense of independence. It was time I found my own path, my own means of self-expression and source of fulfilment. I could no longer afford to rely upon Martin for both my entertainment and security. Yet, each time I reached out in a different direction, my hopes and aspirations seemed to get dashed.

I took up my camera again and began photographing people with more insight and passion. I wanted to experiment, to learn how to convey the subtleties of expressions, to discover that moment when I could capture the essence of someone on film. I started to print my own pictures and gain some understanding of how it was possible to manipulate the subtle tones of images for maximum effect. But my attempts were short-lived. I knew that I could not justify the expense of setting up my own darkroom and I felt uncomfortable relying upon another person for assistance. Anyway, in practical terms it was going to be a hard way to earn a living. There was too much competition out there.

I decided to continue with my education instead. Maybe I would find what I was looking for by attending university and following a more conventional career? I began studying English. I was baffled by Chaucer, exhilarated by Keats and Yeats, but soon became bored with the interminable emphasis upon analysis of the texts. I believed that novels were written to inspire or entertain, not to be pulled apart. And so I moved on. What about history – what was history? Understanding the past so that we could gain more insight into the present. There seemed to be a certain irony about that. The cycle of errors went on and on . . . it seemed that wars and disputes over land and rights would never cease. Were we never going to learn from the mistakes of the past? I doubted it. My studies did not last long.

I went to stay with my sister. She had just had her second child, a little girl called Lucy. I knew that she would appreciate some help and company. As I waded through a pile of ironing I was prompted to ask her advice.

'I've not had a period for four or five months – do you think it matters?'

'Are you pregnant?'

'No, I can't be. I don't feel it anyway.'

'You don't look it. It seems as though you've lost weight rather than put it on! How heavy are you?'

I looked across at her bundled up comfortably on the chair breast-feeding. I had always felt close to her. 'I don't weigh myself any more.'

'If you get too thin, you stop having periods you know.'

'Oh?' I felt confused. 'I didn't know.'

'You must be careful, really. Remember my friend Nel? She was ill for several years because she let herself get too thin. Come on, let's go and cook something tempting to eat – what do you fancy?' And she plonked the baby in my arms and waltzed off into the kitchen.

I adored my sister. She was so good natured and fun-loving – a tonic for anyone. Sometimes I wished that I could be more like her. For her, life was so simple.

Self-denial becomes addictive. At first I cut down on bread and potatoes, then cheese and butter, and then began missing meals. Imperceptibly my weight dropped so that no one really noticed. Only those who saw me irregularly would occasionally remark upon my changed appearance.

The more aware I became of food, eating and meal-times, the more I distanced myself from others. The confusion that lay within myself began to be reflected in the world around me. I began to 'people watch' and, as I did so, I became increasingly contemptuous of the superficiality that took up most of our lives. The less I ate, the more virtuous I felt. I started to believe that society's ills lay at the door of vanity and gluttony. After all, these were the aspects of humankind that turned people into cartoon images when they could have been aspiring to higher things. The more weight I lost, the stronger I felt and the greater my resolve became to carry on with my cause. At least I was sincere in what I was doing – by purging myself, I believed that I would purge society too.

'How little food does one need to survive?' I asked my brother, who was a doctor.

He confirmed my view. 'Very little, a bit of starch and some vegetables or pulses. We all eat far too much.'

I began to see the world in a different way, as an observer, someone who thought themselves to be apart from the fray. I saw myself as a soldier of righteousness. How could I awaken people to the deeper meaning of life? Indeed what was the meaning? Who was I – why was I here? Indeed why were any of us here? Sometimes I recognized a wildness, a madness that was taking hold of me, but I found it exhilarating and was not frightened by its force. I wanted to be free from ordinariness, restriction and constraint. The only way, it seemed, that I could accomplish that was to separate my mind from the physical body, for the body symbolized the world and that was where all problems lay.

My feelings of rebelliousness transcribed themselves into crazy schemes that I persuaded Martin to help me implement. We heard that there were some deserted farmhouses up for tender on the North York Moors – the Forestry Commission wanted to sell them off.

'How about buying one?' I asked him. 'I'd like to live in a forest.'

'I'm sure it would be a sensible investment to put some money into property.'

'We could keep the flat as your London base and I could make our home up north.' I liked the idea of sanctuary; it appealed to my increasing sense of isolation.

In search of suitable properties, I often went alone. On an empty stomach, with escapist fantasies whirling in my head, I drove for miles along high fell roads and remote forest tracks, searching desperately for a home, a refuge where I could settle to contemplate the subtler nuances of life.

Then I decided that I wanted another child.

'Eliza, I don't think you'll be able to conceive.' Martin was realistic.

'I'll go to the doctor. They'll give me something.'

I was sent from one doctor to the next, from one hospital to the next. But they all said the same thing.

'I think that if you put on some weight, your periods might come back.'

'I'm trying, but it's difficult.'

'We can give you a low dose of oestrogen . . . but maybe it would help if you talked to someone, a psychiatrist? I don't think this is just a physical problem.'

I accepted the offer and was transferred to another hospital. I was relieved. I thought I might find someone who would understand. I looked forward to my first visit to the psychiatrist . . . at least I would have someone to talk to.

An appointment was quickly arranged. After the usual preliminaries and a brief résumé of my medical history, Doctor Tonks leaned back in his chair and spoke casually. 'Tell me what you think about yourself . . . your life.'

I was slightly taken aback. 'I don't know. Probably not a lot.' I could not think how to respond to such a question.

'Well, tell me how you spend your time?'

I was reluctant to say that I had spent the previous week chasing around the North York Moors looking at derelict farmhouses, before setting off at four that morning to drive south to meet him . . . in the hope of finding answers.

I decided to be more practical. 'I've done a bit of studying, but it never came to much. I spend most of my time looking after my daughter.'

'Do you have any interests or hobbies? Anything you like doing particularly?'

I looked at him dubiously across the desk. 'I'm not sure. I've tried one or two different things in the past.'

'Do you think there is something missing from your life?'

I knew that he was trying to encourage me to talk, but I could not find any appropriate answers. 'I don't know. I wish I did know, but I don't.'

'Would you say you were happy?'

'I'm not sure what that means.'

'Whether you feel content with the life you are leading at the moment?'

'Presumably not.'

'Do you know why not?'

'I wouldn't be here if I did.'

'Tell me about your husband – do you have a good relationship?'

'My illness has nothing to do with my husband. This is *my* problem – it's to do with my relationship with the world . . . my need for a means of self-expression. I feel bottled up inside,' I said assertively. At least I knew the answer to that question.

I was grateful for his attention. I sensed that he was leading me to the edge of a precipice so that I could get a better view of myself, but the terrain seemed too dangerous. At least he was trying to help. My fortnightly visits became weekly ones. One time I ventured to explain. 'I want to express what's inside me but I can't. I don't know how. I can't reach deep enough down.'

'Maybe if we get you well physically, your mind will become clearer. Your weight is still dropping.'

'Maybe – but . . . ' And there was my dilemma. I would not eat until I had found answers and the more I searched, the more elusive they became.

Meanwhile Martin had achieved his ambition of playing Hamlet. The opening night was in Harrogate and we decided to throw a small party for his agent and some friends in the profession. I had perfected the art of disguising my true physical state. That night I decided to wear a soft green velvet dress that bowed out around my stomach. I had a bath to freshen up. Maybe it was the strangeness of the bathroom, the different arrangement of the furniture . . . for as I got into the water I glimpsed a skeletal figure in the mirror. I was surprised and a little shocked. I quickly lowered myself, wanting to feel the warmth and comfort of the water around me but, as I did so, my bones dug into the bath and it hurt to sit down. Presumably I had no padding left.

The next morning Martin confronted me. 'You're not well are you?' He seemed annoyed . . . irritated by the fact that his wife was ill. He paused. 'What are you going to do about it?'

Maybe it was the suppressed anger in his voice that prompted me to act. I remember faltering as I reached for the telephone. 'Mum,' my words became indistinguishable. 'Help . . . I need some help.'

'Oh my darling, come home, come home . . . '

It was the first time that I could remember asking for help. It felt strange. A part of me was relieved that I had at last been able to show my vulnerability. But another part of me was frustrated that I had suffered for nothing. I still had no answers.

So Rachel and I returned to the comforts and care of my mother. I knew that time was running out. I was going increasingly mad trying to find my sanity. Each day I became more disgusted with my habits, and I hated the hurt that I inflicted on those who were trying to help me. I concealed food, destroyed it, lied about it – did anything rather than eat it. I wanted the tide to turn, but I did not know how to turn it.

I tried talking to my father. 'The trouble is that I have nothing to offer the world.'

'Eliza you have so much.'

'I have no means of self-expression – no talent or expertise.'

'You're a wonderful mother, a good and loyal wife. That means a lot.'

'No,' I protested, 'and even if it were true, I still need something more.'

'Picasso was a genius but he wasn't a happy man. There are many people who find happiness and fulfilment without excelling at one particular thing. I believe they're often the greater men.'

I wanted to tell him that he was one of those.

The next time I went to see Doctor Tonks, he asked if he could meet Martin. During my consultations I had mentioned that Martin viewed illness as weakness and distrusted the idea of my seeking help outside our marriage. Martin believed that he knew best what was right for me and hated the idea of doctors, friends or family interfering with our life together. I waited outside the consulting-room while they talked. When Martin eventually came out, his face was ashen. He stared at the wall in front of him and did not say a word.

'What?' I asked as a way of reminding him that I was still there.

'Let's go.' He spoke sternly.

I pressed him for some information. 'Well what did he say?'

'I'll tell you later.'

I waited until we got into the car then challenged him again. 'I want to know what he said.'

Martin grabbed me by the arms and swung me round to face him. I could see fear in his face. 'Alright then. He said that you weigh less than five and a half stone and you'll die unless you go into hospital. Is that what you want to hear?'

At last, I thought to myself, someone has managed to make him listen. Would he now listen to me?

I fell in love with womanhood and I wanted mine back again. The curves, the fullness, the timeless appeal that never ceases to lure and attract. The soothing voice of care and gentleness that offers hope. The potential for creativity that lies within. Moistness, warmth . . . I wanted to be absorbed by it all, smothered by the feminine, filled with a sense of security. The ideal of Mother stirred me and drew me close . . . the Mother that always gives.

3

I had to learn to eat again, to live again, to choose Life and not run away. I had to let go of aloofness, take part in the furore, climb on the band-wagon and begin to enjoy it. How could I offer myself to the world if I turned my back on it? Had it been my feelings of inadequacy that had caused me to harm myself? Or was it my contempt for materialism that I believed to be a distraction from seeking deeper meaning to life? I was not sure . . . and perhaps it did not matter any more. The desire to get better was there, ready to take me forward into a new phase of my life.

In the late sixties anorexia was still not widely recognized as an illness, and at first it was mooted that I should go into a mental hospital. I shrank from the idea for I now yearned for a sense of normality. A specialist in Cambridge, however, realized that this condition was affecting increasing numbers of women undergraduates and wanted it researched more thoroughly. And so it was that I ended up going into a general hospital under his care, not only because of his personal interest and expertise, but also because Rachel could be cared for by my parents close by.

It took almost a month of hospital nursing, followed by several weeks of convalescence, before the scales were turned around. The professor was kind and encouraged me all he could. 'Go into the hospital kitchen and ask for anything you want at any time. Have your food and enjoy it. That's what you need to do – eat and rest.'

But food was a shock to my system. Each time I finished a meal I lay back physically exhausted, unable to get my breath and with my pulse raced. It felt as though I had just finished a long, gruelling cross-country race. I preferred to stay with the comfort foods – milk puddings, crumbles, cereals and potatoes – which I found easier to digest. I took my recovery seriously, afraid of missing out on any part of the diet that was prescribed me. My face filled out, my cheeks reddened and my arms looked like arms again instead of spindles. Once again I began to move like a young woman instead of an old one. It was a renewed, invigorated Eliza that began to emerge from her ordeal.

As my physical strength returned, my confidence increased too. I realized that I needed more stability if I were not going to be tossed around by life any more. My relationship with Martin offered me little help with that. For me, he represented the positive and negative forces in life. Sometimes he displayed a great capacity for caring, but at other times a darker side of his nature cast a deep shadow over the household that made me feel apprehensive and afraid. Since the beginning of our marriage I had tried to persuade myself that the more positive side of his character would win through, but I was becoming increasingly disillusioned. I found it impossible to cope with his changeable manner and constant mood swings: they left me feeling confused and afraid. Sometimes he was aggressive and violent, other times he made me feel insignificant and worthless. He was a master at manipulating people and events for his own end. Whenever I tried to retaliate, he managed to find yet another way of putting me down – and the same thing would happen again and again.

Yet I was still not sure that I had courage enough to leave. Was it easier to live alongside his unpredictable temper, or face the insecurity of being alone with no income or career prospects? I knew that a final separation would sting but, if I were ever going to find my own centre, I realized that I had to take myself away from him. We had been together for almost five years.

And so it was that I began to look for a home in London for Rachel and me. I charted each area so that I could make an informed decision as to where we could live reasonably, and find a good school for her. After several weeks of searching we went to see a large rambling house in Chiswick. It must have been a mistaken suggestion as it was much too big for the two of us, however we liked it. It was light, airy, overlooked the river and was for sale at a very reasonable price. The fact that it had a leaking roof, woodworm, damp wallpaper that dated back to Victorian times, and a piece of land that was filled with six foot high weeds, was no deterrent.

I could not have possibly afforded the house myself but, when Martin saw it, he fell in love with it. And so it was that by this strange twist of fate we were drawn back together. It did not take much to convince me that bringing up a child with no means of income would be difficult, and I was still of the mind that Martin's moods would level out. I reasoned that the house would mirror the challenge that we faced in our own lives. The physical work would make a welcome change from the pressure of Martin getting acting work, and it would also distract me from past concerns regarding my illness. We were both excited at the prospect of taking on the labour – the joinery, the plastering, the redecoration, the digging of the garden and planting it anew. It would be a fresh start for us both.

Values changed as we immersed ourselves in the task of renewal. It became a time of contemplation about the subtlety of paint colours, wood varnish or the design of ceramic tiles. We loaded up one skip after another with building rubbish and garden debris. And the more mess we cleared out of the house, the clearer we felt within ourselves. Between us we were creating order where before there had been none.

Although our patch of land was small, we wanted to fill it with ornamental bushes, fruit trees, flowers and herbs, so that we could remind ourselves of continental colours and warmth. We planted apple trees, a vine, a climbing pear and peach trees. For our fig we lined a hole with concrete to deter its roots from spreading so that all its energy would be expended upwards and its fruit could be ripened by the English summer sun. In the early evening when the day's work was done, we sat on the terrace, sipped a glass of wine, and surveyed our efforts. We were proud – our patch of wilderness had been tamed.

As the house took on a greater semblance of order we began to entertain friends. One evening John the photographer came to supper. The conversation revolved around the latest films, television dramas, forthcoming theatre productions and what different actors were doing where. Martin often felt threatened by such conversations, believing that he should be doing more. His persistent fear of failure seemed to be the cause of many of his moods. Maybe John sensed the unease around the table – to me the tension was familiar.

'I've just learned to meditate,' he announced unexpectedly.

His words came out of the blue and we fell silent. I was taken aback. Momentarily I was stunned, not just by the change of conversation, but by the word itself – *meditate*. Its vibration penetrated deep within my mind.

After a moment or two John continued: 'Robert taught me. He's just come back from a three month teacher training course with Maharishi in Majorca. He told me it would do me good.' John had suffered from high blood pressure for many years.

'Tell me more.' I could hear the suppressed enthusiasm in my voice.

'It's difficult to talk about it. You really have to experience it. It would do you good Martin – it helps you relax.'

That evening, the veil that had been drawn across my path for so long, was lifted a little . . . just enough to allow a chink of light to shine through. In the utterance of that word *meditate*, it was as though I had been handed a key – a key to myself. Would I now be able to reach down inside myself and discover that part of me that I had sought for so long . . . in so many different ways? Would this be the end of my suffering and confusion?

As I opened the door of the darkened north London room, I seemed to enter another world. It was lit by two candles and burning camphor. I offered some wild flowers, fresh fruit and a new white handkerchief, and Robert laid them carefully on the *puja* table. The sweet smell of incense hung heavy in the air and I was dimly aware that the walls were covered with rich, brightly coloured eastern paintings and batiks. Despite the strangeness of the scene, I felt undisturbed by it. Softly and rhythmically Robert chanted some Sanskrit prayers while moving his hands around a bowl of rice, the camphor light and some water. I was mesmerized by the ceremony, lulled by his voice. Then he turned towards me and whispered a mantra – my mantra, mantra, mantra . . mantra . . mantra. I took the thought inside my head, and meditated for the first time.

In the following days horizons peeled back. A new vision of the world was laid out before me. Whether it was the experience of meditation itself – that profound sense of inner comfort and calm – or the new-found knowledge that I was gleaning from Robert, I was unsure. It was irrelevant anyway. I was discovering that I had access to an inner world – previously unattainable – of such magnitude and beauty that I was amazed and humbled by it all. Why had it taken me so long to arrive at this point? Why was this open secret not more widely known about? Different strands of my life that so recently had been disconnected and confused, came together in one glorious kaleidoscope of pattern and symmetry. Maybe at last, life would begin to make sense.

Robert came to visit us two or three times to make sure that we were meditating properly and to give us some background information. He was tall, lean, fair-haired and had a cheery open face with bright blue eyes. He was playing in a musical in the West End and I imagined him to be a lithe and agile dancer. It seemed slightly incongruous to watch him sitting on the sofa in his jeans and T-shirt, talking coherently about expanding states of consciousness; but I listened to every word.

'All of us are clogged with stresses. We pick them up all the time – good ones, bad ones, indifferent ones – until we get so choked up that we become like an old car that is capable of only chugging along. It's simple. Meditation washes the stresses away. It's as though we're giving our car a good service, oiling it up so that it can run smoothly again.'

'What do you mean by a 'stress'?'

'See it as an impression – an impression that's left on you by any experience that you go through. If you're rigid and set in your ways, it'll cut deep – but if you're free, it's like drawing a line in water and will cause no harm. We want freedom, don't we? And if we meditate we'll get it!'

'How soon?' I asked laughingly.

'Soon enough if you meditate regularly.'

Robert's explanations and ideas about different states of consciousness opened up shutters that had been closed for far too long. No wonder I had felt trapped, isolated in the gloom. Light was now shed on this inner world.

'Universal consciousness is the ultimate experience.'

Robert spoke as if it were just around the corner, something that we could attain in a few weeks time. I began to think . . well, maybe when I am thirty years old . . .

He continued to explain. 'As you meditate, you progress through different states of consciousness. Firstly the mind becomes fully awakened; then everything in the relative world is able to be experienced at its subtlest level; and the final realization comes when you experience that there is no difference between you and everything else. That's Unity. It is the experience that all is One.'

'It sounds good to me,' I said positively. It was difficult to know how to respond to such a concept.

Robert assumed the role of instructor again. 'So just keep on meditating and eventually you'll get there.'

'Where have you got to?'

'In Majorca we meditated for hours on end. Some people went a bit crazy, but the whole idea was to get rid of massive blocks of stress, so that we could progress more quickly.'

'And did it work?'

'As one grows, the changes that happen become part of us – we get used to being our new selves. It's by looking back that I can see that a new Robert has emerged.'

And then he disappeared. It was a while before I saw anything of him again.

During the following months I never missed out on my meditations. These times in the day became my sanctuary. As I pushed back the barriers within myself, I discovered a landscape that was strange and exotic – full of extraordinary images that I wanted to express. With no one to call upon, I tried to reason and explain them to myself, in order to make sense of my new view of the world. Ideas were floating to the surface so fast. I was overwhelmed by different schemes and solutions as to ways humankind could better itself. If people went on looking outwards instead of in, they were ignoring the essence of who they were – their True Self. No wonder there was so much confusion, ignorance and despair in the world. As time went on there were two sides of me that pulled at each other: one part of me wanted to become a revolutionary so that I could uproot the greed and indolence that caused the suffering – and another part of me wanted to become a poet so I could sing about Life's joys and pains.

As an image came into my mind I would remain very still, so that I could experience the silence from which it came. Then, in that state of suspension, I would take up my pen so that I could begin translating the thought into words. By so doing it gave me time to explore it, develop its theme, illuminate it and give it colour and texture. Through the process it crystallized, and a poem or piece of writing would emerge. In this way ideas were given expression, and I was released from their hold.

I began visiting a close friend of my parents who showed interest in my writing and new-found ideas. For me, I was relieved to have someone to talk to. Victor was a scientist, brilliant and versatile, with varied interests and a love of life and its idiosyncrasies.

'Do you know who one of my greatest heroes is?' He would say as he tickled the ivories on the piano, showing off his talent for playing jazz.

'Now, let me see . . . ' I teased, 'Could it be Art Tatum?' I had heard this one before.

'He was a genius – I respect genius. It doesn't matter whether it comes through the piano, painting, a tennis court or the science lab. . . . I admire brilliance. Tell me about your poetry. I'd like to see some.'

'It's hardly of that calibre, but I don't mind showing you.'

'Send me some.'

I liked Victor. Despite his abruptness, he seemed to care. He was intrigued by people's minds and how they ticked. Unlike anyone else I knew then, he took the time to understand me. Over a meal or a glass of brandy he would read my poetry, listen to my ideas, and ask about the effects and benefits of meditation. Together we would philosophize on how the world could be a better place. There was never any contention if my views were quite different from his own, for we were both open and willing to listen and probe. The rare opportunity of being able to talk freely, without restriction, enabled me to discover more about myself and my direction.

Whether it was Victor's fascination with the creative process at work within me, or a conscious recognition of my changed vision of life, I am not sure – but something prompted me to delve deeper into the meditative process. Not only did I want to immerse myself in the experience, but also I wanted to understand more about the philosophical and spiritual aspects. And it seemed that the best way I could do that was to learn to teach it.

The training courses lasted three months, cost a fair bit of money, and there was the added responsibility of making sure that Rachel had some schooling during that time. She was now six. Yet, when I got an idea in my head, I was not one to be deterred by practical obstacles. A car was sold to pay for the training, a small school was established on the course so that children could accompany their parents, and Martin accepted this new interest in my life with equanimity. In fact he positively encouraged us to go. I presumed that our absence for that length of time would give him the opportunity to live free for a while. But I did not mind – at last I had found a passion of my own.

The Belgian coastline is not an inspiring place during the winter months. That year the rainfall was high and the westerlies kept blowing in, but courses were held where accommodation was cheap, so no one complained. In the past, teacher-training courses had been held in beautiful locations and had been regarded as time out from life, but that was no longer the case. They were now periods of intensive tuition, combined with extended meditations in order to deepen one's own inner experience.

Those who had made the necessary sacrifices to be there, were clearly sincere people. They were not only committed to furthering their own personal growth, but also to qualifying as teachers, so that they could pass on the benefits of meditation to others. The regime was strict – every lecture had to be attended, each test and exam passed, and there were to be no parties or sexual exploits. On the positive side there was a wide range of interesting students from different countries, and the vegetarian food was fresh, varied and well-cooked. Time off was spent on the beach, blowing away the cobwebs.

Reminders of the Second World War still haunted the shoreline.

'You can feel the fear that those soldiers went through,' I shuddered.

Libor, a student from Czechoslovakia, was with me at the time. 'This is a place that is littered with memories. Imagine landing here among the sand dunes not knowing whether you're going to last five minutes, half an hour, or long enough to see your girlfriend again.'

'I can't. Facing death straight in the face . . . ' I pondered. 'It's the pain and squalor that would frighten me . . . not the actual dying. That would come as a relief.' I breathed deep to inhale the sea air. 'You can almost taste the sense of desolation here.'

Libor spoke in a matter-of-fact voice: 'If you can face death, you can face life.'

'That takes a lot of doing.'

'Sniff the air and focus your mind on that. Let your thoughts go to the fresh wind blowing in off the sea, the bite, the saltiness. You see? It's invigorating and all memories of the war disappear.'

'Is it so easy for you?' I said laughing.

'No. But we all have bad memories and we cannot allow them to stop us from beginning again. We have to make some effort, that's all.'

'Of course, the invasion of your own country . . . '

I worked hard. I studied my notes thoroughly, learned how to sing the universal peace prayer in Sanskrit, and tried to find out what teaching opportunities there might be when I returned home. I imagined myself setting up a centre and instructing full time; it was time I earned a living. At the end of the course it was customary for Maharishi to visit and give some talks and answer our questions. There must have been several hundred of us there. There was a tradition of garlanding him with flowers when he entered the hall, so each one of us held our specially chosen offering in the hope that we would have the chance of giving him it. The form was that we should bow our heads and say *namaste*.

We were all excited to see him in person, this small, scantily-clad Indian guru with long thinning grey hair and an infectious giggle. I liked his sense of humour and slightly mischievous nature and I was impressed by his philosophy of life. After all I was deeply indebted to him: he had offered me a way out of my confusion and my life had been transformed. The little man meant a lot to me.

His closest disciples stayed near to him at all times, whether he was travelling, teaching or deciding how the meditation practices could reach a wider audience. One day a tall well-spoken young English man approached me.

'Maharishi would like to meet you.'

I was taken aback. 'Why?'

'We've heard you have some friends,' he was obviously grasping for the right words, ' . . . know some people who have influence in politics.'

'So what?'

'Maybe they could help Maharishi get his message across to the world? He would like to talk to you about it. Will you come tomorrow morning when he gives his audience?'

It was as though I was being summoned to meet a royal dignitary but, whatever use my friends may or may not have been, I was curious to meet the man himself. I was not going to refuse the invitation.

I decided to give Maharishi a white rose and, having carefully picked off all the thorns so they would not prick him, I clutched it tight. I was a little apprehensive as I waited for him with the dozen or so others in the small room. No one spoke, a few meditated – I just stared at the empty chair in front of me where he would soon be seated. It was as though we were expecting a momentous event to occur. I was amused by the scene. Eventually the door handle moved, there was a shuffling sound outside and Maharishi was ushered into the room.

Everyone got up, and then they all suddenly dropped to the floor. I followed suit. While down on my knees I squinted at the girl in front of me to make sure that I understood the correct procedure; to my surprise I saw that she had fully prostrated herself. I looked around and saw that others had done the same, so I slid my arms out in front of me and put my head to the ground. I stared at the wooden floorboards, closely examining their colour and grain as a way of distracting myself from my acute feeling of discomfort. Why was I doing this? Was I compromising myself? As far as I was concerned Maharishi was simply a teacher. I wondered why these people were treating him otherwise, making him out to be a saint or something. I certainly did not feel right lying on the floor in front of him and I was relieved when everyone stood up and said their *namastes*.

'I want to see the English lady. Where is she?' He asked in his high-pitched voice.

'I'm here Maharishi.'

'Get the lady a chair. The rest of you can go.' And he waved his hand to implement the instruction.

I felt more at ease sitting alone with him.

'Is the course going well?'

'Yes thank you. I'm enjoying it.'

'You know you must learn very well all the procedures, the checks and the teachings . . . '

'Yes. I'm doing my best.'

'You understand how much these techniques can help everyone. They should be taught in schools, universities, hospitals and businesses. We need to reach out to so many people. I think you can help us, no?'

'I'll certainly try.' I was surprised that he had not asked me anything about myself. After all he was my teacher, and I had so much to tell him about the changes that had happened since I had started meditating – all my new perceptions and understandings.

'You have some friends in politics?'

'Yes.' I was a little hesitant.

'Maybe I could make a video for your friends and you could show it to them. I could explain about the procedures and benefits of meditation. You see, if it were integrated into the political system from the top, then it could be introduced as a matter of course into everyone's lives.'

'I understand what you mean.' I answered courteously, deciding that I would be wasting my time explaining that we live in a free society and that there is the element of choice.

'There are many social benefits,' he raised his voice in excitement. 'If more people meditate the crime rate would go down, there would be better health, improved learning in schools, better performance in business, more creativity, and no need for wars . . . so many things. Even if just a few people start meditating in a village or small town, it has an effect on their whole environment. It radiates out to the others.'

These were the broad claims that I had become familiar with during my training. I had no doubt that Maharishi had complete faith in his practice of meditation.

I felt obliged to respond. 'If you make a video explaining these things, I would be pleased to take it back with me. I'll show it to those people who I think might be interested.' I felt safe with that promise.

'And you must teach your friends to meditate so they have the experience of meditation as well . . . you must remember to learn the training very well.'

Prior to our meeting I had been instructed not to look into his eyes as it would drain his energy. I never quite understood this, as I had frequently been told that Maharishi was a man with limitless energy who had no need of more than two hours sleep a night. Anyway, during our conversation, he had persisted in looking straight ahead and had barely glanced in my direction, so this had not been a problem. My chair had been placed deliberately at an angle.

Unexpectedly, almost as though he had run out of things to say, he tilted his head in my direction and gave a little smile. 'Good,' he said. The interview had come to an end.

I had to get a grip on myself and concentrate. I not only had to cope with my erratic emotions as a result of the extended meditations, but also had a lot of memorising to do. Maharishi wanted his teachers to be word perfect so that the practices were passed on correctly, with least chance of deviation or mistakes. At times I yearned for home and sentimentally thought about Martin. There was still no word from him. Each day I went to the post expectantly, only to come away with my hopes dashed and feelings of tightness twisting in my stomach. I presumed that he had been roaming during my weeks away . . . off with another girl whom I knew nothing about.

It was the not knowing that caused the pain, the wondering whether he was engrossed in work or pleasure, though really I knew it was the latter . . . and that was the reason why he dared not write. Our relationship had deteriorated into a halting affair – a constant to-ing and fro-ing. At times I believed that I was getting stronger and more self-sufficient, but other times I felt as insecure as I had done during the first years of our marriage. Why was I still pouring myself into an illusory relationship that brought more pain than joy? Why was I more frightened of breaking out on my own, than of leaving myself exposed to his unpredictable nature? The answer was simple: I still needed Martin. I began counting the days until my return home. I had not done that since I was at boarding-school.

Martin met Rachel and me at the station. He approached us with a smile. 'God, you look tired! Haven't you had any fresh air?'

'We've been working hard. There hasn't been a day off.'

He took us straight home. It was spring and the trees were just coming into blossom, which added vibrancy as well as fragrance to our little garden. The new foliage looked bright and fresh and made a welcome sight.

We knew that we had to talk; it was Martin who broached the subject first. 'I received your letters.'

'What happened to yours?'

'I don't know. I couldn't bring myself to write.'

'Why not?' I had to play the game even though I knew the answer really. 'I was worried. I waited day after day for some news . . . Rachel would have liked to hear from you.' In such situations I would often use her either for support or self-protection.

'You chose to go off on your course.'

'I had to go and do something for myself – you know that. It was high time I did.' He had obviously regarded my absence as permission to wander.

'Then what's to stop me from going off and doing something for *myself*?'

'It's different. Flings come to nothing. You know that.' It seemed presumptuous of me to be so sure. Maybe he was still living with someone else?

'Your letters were powerful.' He hesitated a little. 'They disturbed me and made me think more carefully about what I was doing. But I have to admit that I'm not living here at the moment. You guessed right . . . there is someone else . . . but I'll always love you too and there lies my confusion. I'm sure I'll be back, but at present I need more time.'

So it had come out into the open. I had always preferred it that way. I gazed across at the old wooden dresser with the willow-patterned plates that decorated it, then out of the window at the flowering clematis, and down to the rush matting on the floor. Yes, I felt more sanguine, calmer about our situation now that I was home. I was in familiar surroundings again, and they helped me to feel more secure.

During the past three months my emotions had run wild. With all the extra meditation I had done, stresses that had been suppressed for years had been brought to the surface. These were experienced consciously as our fears and anxieties. No wonder my relationship with Martin had become a priority in my mind.

It was still through him that I sought my comfort and security. Yet how would I ever find freedom if I persisted in clinging onto him? On meditation courses the process of release was accelerated and this could increase sensitivity – that was why people took themselves away to places of retreat. But, as I had already experienced, once stress had been released horizons were expanded. It was now time to re-order my life and discover what effect the course had had on me. It should not matter whether Martin was with me or not.

Through my role as meditation teacher I had a means of communicating with people from all walks of life. I had wanted this opportunity for so long. I arranged to give regular talks at the local library in which I could explain about the benefits of meditation. At that time there was increasing interest in such ideas and it was not long before I had a steady flow of students coming to the house to learn. They were a mixed bunch who ranged widely in age, career and social background, but each one had in common a desire to gain something more from their lives. All of them were seekers of a kind. As far as I was concerned their particular reason for learning, whether it was for better health or more emotional stability, did not matter. The more I taught, the more I realized that the benefits gained through meditation often appeared in quite a different area from that which had brought them to learn in the first place. The process of diving within held a mystery of its own.

'We're under such a lot of pressure at work,' an airline pilot confided in me. 'We have regular checks on our speed of reaction time, coordination and so on – and I'm getting older. I'm concerned that I might not make the grade.'

I tried to reassure him. 'Meditation is a very effective way of reducing stress levels. It'll help you, I'm sure it will.'

A couple of months after I had taught him, he returned to tell me how he was getting on with his practice.

'You know, since I've started meditating, life has become so much easier at home. My wife and I have actually begun to enjoy each other's company again. We've even been out to restaurants and a film together, and we haven't done that for years. The children notice the change too.'

'I'm delighted. And how about your work?'

'Oh it's much the same as ever. I get to travel and see the world which is more than some people do. I like it . . . never had a problem there.'

Occasionally people who had a long history of psychiatric illness would come to learn. We were warned against taking on such students as it was believed that they would take up too much of our time.

'Please teach me to meditate. I'm sure it'll help. I want peace of mind . . . to get away from all that's going on inside my head. I feel desperate. If I go back to hospital they'll give me electric shock treatment again. I don't want any more of it. Please help me . . . please. It's my last chance.'

He was a man in his mid-forties who had been in a steady job until his wife left him. At that point his life had crumbled around him. Maybe I was gullible, maybe he was a genuine case – it was always difficult to know. But there was something about his manner that made me feel that he was a genuine seeker – someone who really had no one to turn to for help. I thought that some brief periods of meditation spread out through the day might give him a refuge. He needed a place of security that he could return to regularly. I finally agreed to teach him on condition that he would do exactly what I said. I explained the procedure. 'You must only meditate for three or four minutes at a time, otherwise it will be too powerful an experience for you. We have to make sure that the stress is neutralized gently, so its release won't cause you any pain. You've suffered so much personal trauma and I'd like to see you benefit.'

When he came to learn he brought a large bunch of wild flowers. His quiet and humble manner endeared him to me and I sensed his appreciation and gratitude for what I was doing. I believed that he would follow my instructions conscientiously and my supposition proved correct. After a few months of meditation, punctuated by regular checks from me, he said: 'I feel I have some peace in my life now. I'll never forget what you've given me.'

My teaching brought me fresh understanding with each student that came, whether it was a social worker that sought greater balance in his life or an Indian woman who wanted to deepen her experience of her own culture. I regarded it a privilege to be able to offer such a wide variety of people the experience of that part of themselves that they knew so little about – the Inner Self. Each week a group of us would gather together to meditate, drink tea, and talk about different aspects of spirituality, religion and life. We gave ourselves the freedom to explore all the doubts and questions that arose in our minds, without feeling restricted or judged. These became precious times when we had the opportunity of discovering more about ourselves and each other. It was as though the windows of our minds were thrown open and fresh air could blow in.

Martin returned home during the summer. Old passion (and presumably need) still ruled. I was glad to have him back, even though it was never easy resuming our relationship after a period of absence from each other. Familiarity and companionship are strong pulls for two people who are still not sure of their direction in life. I valued his support as I got more involved with teaching, and he was drawn to the comforts of home by way of contrast to the increasing insecurity he faced from his profession.

My maternal instincts were also returning. It occurred to us that we could have another child and become a family again. It would be a new beginning, and provide us with another reason for getting back together again. This time it would be a planned pregnancy. Rachel was now seven years old and could do with some companionship . . . someone to care for. I also wanted to show that I was truly well again. I was beginning to realize the extent to which I had abused my body. Had it all been a dreadful mistake, a selfish stance that I had taken against the world and it was now that I was going to suffer the consequences? Did I deserve the chance of being a mother for a second time?

I waited impatiently to see if my body would respond, counting days and waiting for them to go by. Though I had started having irregular periods again, I was worried that I had left it too late . . . that I was all dried up. So it seemed like a miracle when I conceived. The magical force of procreation had taken hold inside me once more, and I was moved by feelings of deep gratitude.

I experienced extraordinary tranquillity, an all-embracing joy, while I carried the child. I glided through my pregnancy effortlessly, believing that my meditation was the reason for this ease. Not once was my teaching interrupted. Indeed, my students were amused. 'Just imagine going to a talk on meditation and being faced with a hugely pregnant woman in a long flowery dress. I was so surprised that I had to find out more.'

Martin was away filming for a television series when I was due to give birth. The doctors decided that because of my rhesus negative blood group, I had to be induced early: I was accumulating antibodies that were affecting the baby. It took a long while for my labour to get under way. After hours of lying on a hard bed in the delivery room wired up to different machines, the doctor saw that I was losing strength. 'I need to get a large steak down you to give you some energy.'

'I'm vegetarian. Anyway are you surprised I'm tired? I've been here for hours.'

'OK – get her a glucose drip and we'll speed things up.'

As the contractions increased in frequency and strength, the pain became more intense and violent. But by then I felt too weak to handle it and I cried out for some relief. As the pethidine took effect, the pain retreated like ebbing waves and I was able to drift away to a place where there was none. The urge to push suddenly brought me back – the hard bed, the sterile white room and, at the end of my bed, a sea of young faces that stared down at me.

'Who are they? What are they doing?' I asked in amazement.

'Student doctors who have come to watch.'

'But there are so many of them.'

'That's how they learn.'

'Don't you ask?' But I ceased to care as the determination to give birth took over.

I held Abigail for a moment or two before she was whisked away to be put into an incubator and intensive care. The next few days faded into each other, as I spent my time moving from the ward to the special unit, and back to the ward again. I wanted to spend as much time with Abigail as possible. In intensive care, soothing music was played to soften the atmosphere and give the babies a sense of comfort and peace. It felt so pure and still in there – everything was pristine, unsullied by earthly mess. And there was so much love that was focused on the sick and premature babies by the mothers and nurses. Little Abigail seemed to me like a study in perfection. I would sit there for hours watching her sleep. Her face radiated an innocence and beauty of a kind that I had not witnessed before.

'She's still in heaven.' The nurse said smiling across at her.

'I reckon you're right.'

'She'll have to join us soon enough.'

' . . . and she'll get a shock when she does,' I remarked as if sensing the imminent future.

After a few days, Abigail's blood count steadied and she was finally allowed back onto the ward. I had longed to have her with me but, during our first night together, she would not settle and I became concerned. 'What do you think the matter is?' I asked the large, rather intimidating Sister on duty.

'I think you should be finding that out for yourself.'

And so I tried feeding, winding, changing, rocking and even singing to her, but nothing would calm her.

'Please Sister, I'm worried. What can I do for her? She might be feeling the change from the special unit to the ward.'

'Then I'll take her to the nursery.' And she marched away with the baby under her arm.

I lay back on the bed physically and emotionally exhausted. I had been awake most of the night. It was a salutary reminder of how slowly the hours pass when one is trying to comfort a restless child. I looked out of the hospital window and saw the first rays of sunlight break through between the tower blocks. Nights seem so long when one is left to cope alone.

The Sister startled me from my reverie. 'Your baby was cold. Didn't you realize that? She needed wrapping up tight that's all.'

We were still in hospital when Martin finished filming; he showed his annoyance by refusing to visit us. His frustration with his acting career was increasingly affecting home life as his temper more often than not got the better of him.

I tried to explain: 'I can't come home until Abigail is better. The doctors won't let her out and I'm not going to leave her.'

'That's ridiculous – she's perfectly alright now. You can discharge yourself.'

'How can I do that? If anything went wrong I would never forgive myself.'

The nurses noticed that I was getting increasingly anxious and upset. My grandmother had just died which meant that my parents were preoccupied with funeral arrangements. Days had gone by and I had had no visitors.

'Would you like to see a social worker?'

'No, I'm fine.' I was adamant. 'My husband just wants me to go home.'

'I think you need some support.'

'No I don't. I'll manage . . . I've managed before.'

How often in my life had I experienced a desire to break out. Time had moved on and, not only had circumstances changed, but I had changed too.

It was now a breaking apart that I was about to witness – a breaking up of such force that I had no power to stop it. I was about to be swept up and carried along by a wave of energy that was far greater than me, that knew its course more accurately. I did not have the strength to stand in its way, but to let go is scary. Fear of the unknown holds one back.

4

Disillusionment is an insidious process that gradually eats its way into a person's life. When the holes get big enough, it may even break it apart. I began to feel as though I was being infiltrated from all sides, and I no longer had the strength to prevent the process from taking place. I was aware that my outer walls, which for years I had used for protection, were in danger of crumbling.

Through teaching meditation, I gained a sense of satisfaction from helping people attain a sense of ease and stability in their own lives. But there was another aspect of my work that made me feel restless. By its nature, meditation allows a process of self-development to occur that is individual and spontaneous: the insights and benefits that I had gained contrasted with those of others. And it was this essential difference between our experiences that made the process of self-development such a mystery. It was here, in that unknown quantity, that the spiritual heralded its presence and demanded attention. I wanted to discover more.

I was beginning to doubt, however, that the organization through which Maharishi had brought his meditation practices to the west, would be able to satisfy that desire to know more. It had become a vast machine, dedicated to the principle of teaching as many people as possible. As time went on, more and more dictates were being imposed on its teachers. New claims were being made that it was our responsibility to move humankind towards an age of enlightenment; and I disliked passing information on to others that I was not sure of myself. By its very nature, rigidity can end up stifling spiritual unfoldment and impeding individual growth. The wheels that turned the organization contradicted my own experience and I preferred to rely on my own intuition for answers. I decided to go on a teachers' course to resolve my doubts.

'Great to see you. How are you doing?' I said excitedly, catching sight of a young Canadian teacher who had helped run my teacher-training course. It was reassuring to see old friends again and we had always got on well.

'Hello,' he said flatly.

And that was all I got. Barely a glance in my direction, not a smile, no connection or conversation. Where was all the laughter, the jokes that we had shared in Belgium? Where were his warmth and sense of humour? I assumed that he had been told to focus on his duties and not get distracted by visiting teachers. It had been rumoured that some close devotees had become celibate, so perhaps that was the situation in his case. Whatever the reason, he had changed and I distrusted his present manner. His head had clearly been turned in the direction of Maharishi and his cause, and I presumed that nothing was allowed to come between him and that – not even common courtesy.

I was confused. If expansion of consciousness meant losing the human touch – that essential quality that makes us who we are – then I was not sure that I wanted it. To me love and kindness were far more important than the ability to be dedicated to any cause, be it one's own or someone else's. I had understood that meditation promoted self-reliance and individual responsibility, and these were attributes that I both admired in others and sought within myself. I distrusted teachers or leaders who attempted to persuade their followers to think or act in the way that they wanted. It smacked of cultism and danger signals flashed in my mind.

The following day it was explained that we had to increase our teaching fees as more money was needed to transmit Maharishi's message to the world. Although we were given guidelines to follow, I had always preferred to make payment a flexible issue, as people's situations varied so much. From now on it seemed that I would have to be stricter. Certainly I had always tried to be a conscientious teacher. In accordance with Maharishi's wishes I had even passed the video tape on to my good listening friend Victor, who at the time seemed the most appropriate recipient. He was a member of the 'Think Tank', an independent body that had been set up by the government to advise on policy. Its members were a diverse group of intellectuals from varying backgrounds who, it was hoped, would bring fresh vision to old and complex problems.

'What did you think of the tape?' I asked him. I had not seen it myself.

His reply was noncommittal. 'Interesting.'

'Anything else?' I sensed that he was trying to be tactful but I wanted his reaction. 'What does he want you to do? What is he asking for?'

'Tell me what Maharishi is like.'

'I'm not sure . . . I can't really say that I know him. He has a sense of humour – that comes across in his teaching.'

'Well there you are then.'

'What do you mean?'

'The tape . . . it's been made by someone with a sense of humour rather than a sense of reality.'

We both laughed and the conversation came to a close. I never mentioned it again.

I am not sure what finally made me leave the organization. I realized that I would have to give up teaching, and that once I had left I would never be allowed back. But my group of meditators offered me their support. They respected the fact that I was acting according to my conscience. I was left to conclude that while the meditation practices themselves offered people inner peace, fresh vision and greater stability in their own lives, the medium through which they were being transmitted to others was becoming more questionable. As I was a part of that process, I believed that I had no choice but to go. I realized that I would miss my students, but I consoled myself with the fact that I would have more time to pursue other interests. Or would I?

Martin was inextricably bound up with life at home and, increasingly, was stamping his mark upon it. When a person feels that they have little control over one aspect of their life, it is often the case that they will assert themselves over another. As Martin's career became more uncertain, he sought his stability by taking charge at home. Over a period of time I became aware of how little choice I had in the way I spent my time. Whenever I tried to express an idea or opinion it led to raised voices and unpleasant contretemps. I disliked the children hearing us argue so I chose to follow the path of least resistance, which usually meant acquiescing. I rarely said what I thought nor dared to act spontaneously. In fact, I ceased to be myself. All I did was to conduct myself in such a way that would cause least upset. No doubt my behaviour must have seemed strange to those who knew me, but I was living in the shadow of my own fear – and I bitterly despised my inability to resolve the situation. I still lacked both the courage and conviction to do so. I now recognized that I was imprisoned in a box of my own making and because of it, my suffering was my responsibility.

In the evenings when Martin went out, I began to get acquainted with a side of myself that I did not know. Having lived with the same person since my late teens, I had lost touch with what pastimes and tastes were my own. Indeed, they had never really had time to mature in the first place. So, whenever I had the chance, I began the task of rediscovering myself. I turned off the television, put on the stereo, and listened to Beethoven or Bach instead. I cooked a simple meal of fresh vegetables onto which I ladled a creamy cheese sauce and, when supper was done, I would take up a book of paintings and become absorbed in the colours and themes. Is this what I would do if I lived alone? I was surprised at how little I knew myself.

The rest of the time I lived a lie. My different guises supported me through the day as I persisted in concealing my true feelings. My performance highlighted life's incongruity. Why did fear have such a strong hold on me? How could it prevent me from being me and expressing myself? Rachel could see through my failing act and Abigail could pick up on my feelings of discomfort. At a few months old her sixth sense was not swamped by the complexities of daily living . . . unlike mine. Surely change had to come soon.

So it was with curiosity that I picked up an envelope with an unusual postmark on it. The letter was from a well-respected American meditation teacher – Walter Bellin. He told the story of a spiritual teacher from South Africa, whom he had heard about recently:

Dear Eliza,

I think you will be interested to hear about a teacher called Gururaj Ananda Yogi from Capetown. Apparently he is regarded as someone of great wisdom and compassion, not only among fellow Asians, but also within the black and white communities there. I'd like to tell you his story.

He was born in Gujerat, northern India, into a business and farming family. As a child he showed a remarkably advanced state of consciousness. When he was only three years old he began asking questions about the meaning and purpose of life, and when he was five he ran away from home to seek an experience of communion with the Divine. Apparently he wandered from village to village for four and a half months visiting many temples and holy men. His parents were frantic with worry and, when eventually they found him, he was ragged, barefoot and miserable. He explained that he had been to all these different temples, but the gods were lifeless and would not speak to him.

As he grew older his desire to experience a Reality far greater than his own remained as strong as ever. He read widely to find out more and, using his highly developed intuition, he became increasingly aware that what he sought lay not only in himself but within all human beings. He came across many names for this greater Reality – the Kingdom of Heaven Within, the Universal Mind, the Real or True Self, the Super-conscious Mind. Yet he also realized that those who experienced this state of being knew that the names used to describe It were of little significance. It was the experience itself that mattered.

He understood that the experience of super-conscious awareness lay buried beneath layers of mental conditioning, and realized that he had to find a way of cleansing the muddy strata of the mind. He knew that he needed meditation practices more powerful than anything that he had practised before, and also a spiritual guide whom he could trust. At fifteen he left home once again visiting numerous ashrams and holy places, in search of a teacher who he believed could help him realize the nature of his True Self. Finally, after a year of wandering, his search ended when he found Swami Pavitrananda in a monastery near Almora in the Himalayas. After a period of intensive and careful preparation under the guidance of his new master, Gururaj reached the critical point in his spiritual development where he was ready to experience full illumination.

One hot Thursday afternoon, Pavitrananda called Gururaj over to him, casually suggesting they should sit together in the garden: 'Let us meditate a few moments,' he said to his pupil. Immediately Gururaj went into profound meditation and merged within a state far beyond the realms of space and time – Universal consciousness. It was an experience of unending joy, eternal freedom and immense peace that transcended all the limitations and patternings of the mind. When he emerged from meditation two hours later, he opened his eyes and everything around him was covered in gold.

Having finally entered a state of Self-realization, Gururaj perceived with utmost clarity that it made no difference how one arrived there, as long as the chosen way was appropriate for the particular individual. Indeed a person's path might not necessarily involve religious affiliations at all. He saw that it was the depth of sincerity, motivation and personal commitment that was of crucial importance.

At that point Gururaj would have been content to stay in an ashram in the Himalayas, but Pavitrananda told him that their roles were different. Gururaj was to immerse himself in the *complexities of daily life in the western world: he was to follow the householder path. By doing so he would experience all the problems, pleasures and pains that ordinary people live through, so that he could help them to go beyond them and achieve inner freedom and fulfilment. As a result Gururaj moved to South Africa, became a successful business man, married and had three children. He then renounced this way of life so that he could become the spiritual teacher he is today.*

Over the years Gururaj has come to realize the value of personal meditation practices. As he says, everyone is a unique individual and has different needs. To be fully effective, the practices must fit into a person's life style and enhance every area of their life.

Gururaj insists that he is an ordinary human being, no different from anyone else, other than the fact that he has walked the spiritual path to its goal. He says that what he has attained, other people can attain too. With this understanding he is treated with no more fuss or reverence than that required by the inherent dignity of any person. In other words, he is one of us.

If you want to know more . . .

I sat down and folded the letter carefully. I was puzzled. Only a few weeks ago I had abandoned my commitment to a meditation movement, and now I was being told about a teacher who acknowledged the benefits of people following their own path. There was something in the story that stirred me. Perhaps here was the spiritual dimension that I had been looking for? After all, my search was not going to end here . . . by its very nature it would never end. How could it? I decided that I wanted to find out more.

In the event I was among the first handful of people in England to learn Gururaj's form of meditation. He had asked Walter, the letter-writer, and Gita, whom he had met in South Africa, to pass on the individual practices. The teaching was a light-hearted affair. We laughed as Walter searched for guidance. 'I haven't a clue what I'm supposed to do next. His next lot of instructions haven't arrived in the post! But how about . . . ' And it seemed to work.

Other times there was an experience of such depth and profundity that there seemed no need for any clarification or understanding. Gita whispered me my personal mantra and, later, confided in me that its power seemed so great that it was as though it reached out to all the corners of the universe. She said that Gururaj had sent a message: *'Beloved one, welcome home . . . '* He then went on to say something about there being a conflict in my life that needed resolving – but I was at a loss to know what he meant.

During the following months my life turned upside down. It was no wonder that occasionally I cried out for help. At times I found myself lying on the bed, threshing my arms about in a wild and irrational manner: 'What am I doing? Why am I doing this to us?'

Martin was confused. 'I don't understand you any more. During the last few weeks you've changed.'

It was true. I had. For a start I had found the courage to implement change. Whether this was finally prompted because Martin raised his hand to me when I was holding Abigail, I am not sure. But the occasion scared me and suddenly I found the strength within myself to act. Could my new-found courage be linked to the personal meditation practice?

I began by calling a solicitor: 'If I were to leave my husband, how much money would I be entitled to from the house? We both contributed towards it.'

After several minutes of prevarication on his part, I grew impatient and tried to pin him down. 'What about half each?'

'That would keep it simple and save on fees, but there are so many issues involved, considerations to make . . . '

But I gave him no chance to elaborate. 'I don't want any fuss. Half each sounds fine.'

I realized that with the amount of money that was due to me, I would never be able to afford a reasonable property in London; so I went to the local library to look at picture books of northern

England. I had heard that property was cheaper up there. At once I was drawn to some old photographs of the Lake District. It looked wild and picturesque and reminded me of the Beatrix Potter books that I had read to my children over the years. The idea of moving 'over the hills and far away' appealed to my inherent romanticism. I telephoned the main post office in Kendal to obtain the name of a newsagent so I could get hold of a local paper. Within days it arrived and I began scanning it for suitable properties. One stood out . . . no doubt because of its name: Woman's Land was situated in Dentdale. I mused that since it was a woman with two daughters who would be moving there, it might be appropriate. I asked the estate agent for details.

'It's a stone built farmhouse that's been renovated, but it's selling cheaper because the owner wants to keep the barn next door to it.'

'What's Dentdale like?'

'The property is about two miles from the village up a back lane. There are just a few farms up there, some fields – it's quite remote really. It's on the western side of the Yorkshire Dales.'

Although I was familiar with the North York Moors, I had never been to the Lake District and had only once visited the Dales from the east. For me this was new country. My sister Teresa, always a good companion in such situations, came with me to see it.

'How many miles are we away from London now?' I wanted to put distance between me and my past.

'Two hundred . . . but there's quite a bit further to go yet.'

'Good. I want to be far, far away.'

It was a June day and, as we broke away from the motorway to wind our way along the country lanes, I was surprised at how green and lush the Dales were. There had been the odd shower that morning which had freshened up everything. As we passed through the village of Dent I was intrigued by its cobbled streets and how small it was. Just as we had been told, a couple of miles further on was Woman's Land, a white-washed farmhouse set back from the road. Teresa and I sat in the car and looked at it. She spoke first. 'It's in a beautiful position, but it's miles from anywhere. You can't live here – I couldn't.' She sounded concerned.

'Come on, let's see inside,' I said hurriedly. I did not want her to influence me before I had seen the property.

The first thing that struck me was how many different families must have lived and worked here over the years; the farmhouse was probably three or four hundred years old. The previous owner had painted the inside walls white, and there were fitted, beige carpets on the floors that made the place feel warm, bright and welcoming. It was a house made up of tilted floors, oak beams and thick stone walls with views of fields, hills and sheep. I peered out of the landing window – the surrounding fells were rounded and gentle and somehow appeared comforting considering that it was so remote. The place was different to anything I had known before, but it felt like home. I mused to myself that no one could ever own a place as full of age and character as this. All we would ever be were passers-by.

We made the journey back as far as Teresa's home in Birmingham, stopping only once to buy some wine. 'Are you really going to live there?' She asked in astonishment.

'I want to.'

'What will you do? You've no money or work. You'll never find another man up there.'

I was amused by her sense of priorities. 'Come on – that's not what I'm moving for.'

'I tell you, you'll be wanting some company on those long winter evenings before long . . . believe me.'

'I'll find some work eventually, but I don't want to leave the children while they're still young and the place is new. We'll manage if we live cheaply – pancakes, lentils, homemade bread . . . that kind of thing. I'm good at it.'

'I know you are – but you're not thirty yet and you're turning your back on life just because your marriage has ended. It may be beautiful, but it's wild up there. I couldn't stand it.'

'Teresa, we're very different – I know this move is right for me.'

When I arrived back in London, I realized that Martin was

bewildered by the pace of events. His mood changes and temper were becoming more unpredictable and I never knew what to expect next. At times he was encouraging, recognising that my move north would enable him to have his freedom down south, whilst also having a place in the country to visit his family. Other times he was infuriated by my impulsive behaviour and would object violently. It was as though he was enslaved my such powerful emotions that at times it seemed that he was completely out of control.

'You never used to be so adamant,' he shouted out.

On that he was right. It was as though I was being driven to make telephone calls, visit the library, drive north, look at Woman's Land, to move away . . .

'It's about time I became more sure of myself.' I did my best to remain calm, but this strategy often made him angrier.

'You can't just leave me like this.'

'Why not?'

'What's going to happen to me – the children?'

'The children will be fine with all that countryside to run around in. You can see them whenever you like.'

'You're behaving completely out of character.'

'I'm sure that this is best for all of us.'

'You make me so angry when you talk like that. How can you possibly know what's best for me?'

'I don't. But I know that if I am the cause of your anger, then it's time that I took myself away from you.'

I had come to the conclusion that if I accepted full responsibility for the situation, I would place myself in a stronger position.

'You really have changed haven't you?'

'Have I?'

There was nothing more to say.

I was beginning to realize that it is by taking risks that we manage to free ourselves. Fear had restricted me for too long. Fear had not only prevented me from breaking out on my own, but it had also been the dictate of my behaviour in the household – my life of cowering and pretence. Yes. I was afraid of oppressive atmospheres and strong negative emotions, but I was also afraid of living alone without money or work. Learning to accept the boundaries that life offers may seem noble at the time, but there is a danger of growing in on oneself. I had been trapped by my own fear for too long. It was time to push back the frontiers and break out of my mould.

I had experienced the power of that creative energy that rose up from within; I had seen the effect that it could have on one's life. I sensed that it was this force alone that could penetrate the polluted waters of the mind and wash away the debris that had accumulated over the years. I did not want to remain a prisoner of murk and mud when I knew there was so much light and space within. I wanted to experience it and absorb it into my life. It was this powerful inner force that drove me on and, when my little self began to intervene with its habitual doubts and queries, I was no longer afraid to ask for help.

'Walter, is it right to take myself away from Martin? Sometimes I feel confused.'

'You must write to Gururaj and ask him for help. He may not write a reply, but he will send you an answer somehow.'

Not long afterwards I received a message from him:

> She must imagine herself to be in a large ship at sea. She has travelled across the seas for many years, but the ship has been set on a course towards northern ice-bound waters. It was heading for icebergs, some clearly visible above the water but others hidden beneath. The ship's course had to be changed so that it might sail away from these cold and barren seas towards the warmth of milder waters. Here life could grow and expand in the sunshine. Sunshine helps growth. Ice and snow inhibit it and create frigid, stagnant situations.
>
> Yet the course of the ship cannot be changed in the twinkling of an eye. The ship has to be turned very slowly. A passenger with no landmarks to guide him might well think that he is continuing on the same course, so imperceptibly is the bow being turned. The first sign that the ship in sailing in the opposite direction will be a gradual change of climate. The ice

begins to melt and the warmth of the sun is felt. Yet many clouds still remain. The destination is not yet reached and much sailing still has to be done. But the passenger must be of good cheer, for the ship is at last sailing on the right course.

When I finally left London with Rachel and Abigail in the back of the car, it was dusk and raining hard. Suddenly the lights on the car went out and the windscreen wipers stopped working. The motorway was heaving with rush-hour traffic and, filled with horror at the thought of being able neither to see nor be seen, I swerved over to the hard shoulder in a frantic attempt to retreat from the fray. A car immediately pulled up behind me and a man got out.

'Are you in trouble?'

'Everything's gone – lights, wipers the lot.'

'It must be a fuse, perhaps more than one. Do you have any spares? I'll see to it.'

Without any fuss, he fixed the problem. I thanked him and went on my way. But the incident gave me faith that whatever problems I was to face in the future, help could turn up in the most unexpected guise. If I was not to be thrown by adversity, I had to learn to trust.

The day I moved in to Woman's Land, we approached the house from the top of the dale under storm-filled clouds that scudded across the sky. The fells were open and untamed, and I could hardly believe the immense sense of space. Surely here I could not fail to build up courage when I was faced with all this wildness day in, day out? It inspired and refreshed, and blew away all the pretence that had become so much part of my life in the south. Here I would be free to discover who I was and begin to express it. My flesh tingled with excitement while my mind reeled with imaginings about the future. Surely I would find happiness here?

We quickly settled into our new life. Each morning Rachel waited at the bottom of the track to catch the bus to the primary school in the village. On the first day she relinquished her southern accent for a gentle Cumbrian lilt. It was natural that she wanted to fit in. The local children welcomed the new face and would often walk the couple of miles up the dale to see her. Together they would make dens up the fell and play in the streams. Abigail, who had just learned to walk, experimented on the uneven ground around the house, tumbling constantly as she chased the few hens that had been left by Brett, the previous owner. He came each weekend to visit his barn and plan its conversion. Patiently he took time to explain how I should unclog the water tank when it got silted up, and remove the snow from the roof rafters when it blew in through the slates. When the moon was full and the sky was clear, I wandered out into the garden to absorb the dale, hardly believing how light it was at midnight. Apart from the occasional hoot from the owls, everything was silent and still. Yes – Dentdale was indeed a magical, mystical place.

By a strange turn of events, my first visitors were Martin . . . and his new girlfriend Susie. She was playing opposite him in a play that was touring the north. I mulled over my responsibilities regarding him and our children. I knew that access was important and I wanted our separation to be smooth and easy, so I decided that I should offer them both a place to stay for a few days. I also wanted to find out how I felt about him after the turmoil of the last few months. From past experience I knew that it was easier to cope with his girl-friends once I had met them, rather than them remaining a figment of my imagination. If the visit was going to be awkward for me, it was certainly going to be likewise for Susie. So I admired her for accepting the invitation.

But as soon as I met her I liked her. Her tousled fair hair framed an unusually long and well-structured face. She had high cheek bones, wide blue eyes and a beautifully defined mouth. Considering the strangeness of the situation that we found ourselves in, she appeared natural and unforced and I liked her fun-loving nature. It was not long before we were able to joke together that at least Martin had good taste in women!

When they both returned home from the theatre at night, I heard them settling into the bedroom next door and I wondered at my feelings. Yes . . . those familiar twinges of pain that I knew so well still pulled at my chest. I was unsure whether they were pangs of jealousy or loneliness. When would they finally let me go? I resented their persistent hold on me. They served as a reminder that despite all the changes I had made in my life, I was still a prisoner of my emotions.

I had been living in the north for a couple of months when I heard that Gururaj was planning a visit to England, to give some talks and run a weekend residential course near London. I wanted to go. I was curious to meet this man whose meditation practices had seemingly spurred me on to change my life. I made plans to journey south and leave the children with their father for a few days.

The course was to be held at a Catholic retreat house. When I arrived I was shown to a single room that had a Bible by the bed and a crucifix on the wall above. I liked the quiet austerity of the place, its simple decoration and carefully tended gardens. There must have been about fifty of us there, all having been involved in some or other meditation group prior to finding out about Gururaj and his individual practices. There was a strange atmosphere amongst us – a mutual acceptance that none of us were there to enjoy a quiet weekend away from the rigours of daily life. No. We were there because we wanted to test, assess and evaluate our new teacher. Many of us were committed seekers who had been disappointed before. We had no intention of being disillusioned again.

We did not have to wait long to see him. It was planned that Gururaj was to give a talk during the first evening and we could ask him any questions we liked. We assembled in the small conference room and I was glad to find a seat near the front. I wanted to get a good view of him. I noticed someone behind me had a flower.

'I never thought of bringing one. I didn't think we had to,' I commented.

'I thought it was tradition.' She said raising her eyebrows questioningly.

We sat quietly and waited. Suddenly the door opened and Walter and Gita came in, accompanied by a jaunty little man with short greying hair who was dressed in an Indian round-necked suit. I was surprised at his appearance though I was not sure why. Maybe it was because he did not fit with my idea of what a spiritual teacher should look like. With an obvious spring in his step he headed straight for the armchair that had been set on a podium in front of us. On his way up, the girl with the flower managed to catch his attention and give it him.

'Thank you,' he said courteously. On reaching the platform he took off his shoes and settled himself cross-legged on the chair.

'Shall we meditate a few moments?'

After a few minutes he murmured, '*Aum shanti, shanti,*' and we opened our eyes. He was wishing us peace.

During the following hour I observed Gururaj closely as he handled the questions that he was bombarded with from the floor. Sometimes they were direct and challenging, other times they appeared to contain anger or resentment. It was apparent that many of them were being voiced as a result of some past hurt. But Gururaj's reactions interested me more than what he actually said. He was straight-forward and easily intelligible, never dodging an answer or evading an issue. Each time he spoke, his words struck a resonant chord deep inside me, as they seemed to emanate a truth that I had not witnessed or heard before. As the hour passed I felt increasingly calm and clear. There was no sharp edge that was left to grate or jar. Instead there was a sense of peace that washed over and through me. Here was a man who appeared to understand us only too well; he wanted to allay our suspicions instead of persuading us to believe. That evening I felt that he genuinely wanted to lighten our load.

There was another thing that caught my eye. While he talked he played with the flower that had been given to him, first taking off its petals, then stamens until there was nothing much left of it. At first this might have have been construed as an unwarranted act of destruction . . . an unexpected thing for a spiritual teacher to do. But it became apparent that there was a deeper meaning to his action: he clearly did not want us to feel obliged to give him flowers or garland him. He had come to help us, not to demand special treatment or feigned subservience. No. He was just an ordinary human being like the rest of us. In taking apart the flower he was showing us that he was no 'pedestal guru'.

In the time I was to spend with Gururaj, I realized how much there was to be gained from trying to understand the reasons why he behaved as he did. At first I wondered why he could not tell us straight, but instead chose to convey his teachings through actions and games. But I soon realized that there was method to his ways. The process of spiritual unfoldment is one of *Self-realization* – in other words we had to uncover the Truth for ourselves. The process of transformation occurs deep within the mind and the spoken word can only touch the surface level. So, the most effective way that Gururaj could penetrate the muddied waters of our minds, was to engineer situations in which we had to look for our own answers. And the deeper we probed, the more we opened ourselves up.

It was not long after I returned home that I was asked whether Gururaj and one or two people who were travelling with him, could come and stay at Woman's Land for a few days. Apparently he was due to give talks in Carlisle and the Lake District and it was thought that Dentdale would make an ideal base.

'You'd be very welcome, but how many of you are there?' I was flustered by the suggestion. 'The house isn't very big and there are the children. Abigail's only a year old and she might disturb him.'

'Don't worry about that. We'll bring extra pots and pans, bedding and plenty of food to cater for us all. As long as Gururaj has a bed, that's all that matters. The rest of us can use floor space.'

It was difficult to refuse such a suggestion and secretly I was flattered at being asked. The truth was that I was concerned about having a guru to stay in the house. I had not the slightest idea what his needs, likes and dislikes would be. Maybe he would want lengthy meditation periods alone, special food, private discussions with the teachers who were coming with him. As the house was not large enough to accommodate these eventualities, I asked Brett if we could use the loft in his barn next door. 'No problem,' he agreed readily. And I was consoled by the thought of more space.

In the event I need not have worried. The days that Gururaj stayed were probably some of the least demanding I have had in terms of entertaining guests. Perhaps that was because no entertaining needed to be done. We lived as a family, helping in the kitchen, eating meals together, going for walks and playing with the children. We talked late into the night about different aspects of life, and perceptions of God in the various countries we lived. The days passed quickly and I was often surprised at how relaxed we were when Gururaj was around. There was no formality or fuss. The only thing we had to be aware of was his need for rest. I had heard that he had been born with a congenital heart defect; and the previous year he had undergone a major heart operation. Prior to this, the doctors in South Africa had been amazed that he had lived so long without surgery. It was when he came out of hospital that he knew it was time to relinquish his business interests and embark on his life as a spiritual teacher.

Before each meal Guruji – as he now asked us to call him – sang the universal prayer for peace. Afterwards we put our hands together and said *namaste*.

'Do you know what it means?' Typically Guruji wanted us to understand the reason for our actions.

Gita volunteered. 'I salute the Divinity within you.'

'Yes. You must remember that it is the thought behind the action that is important, not the action in itself. Thought is more powerful.'

'Then we'd better take care of what we're thinking when you're around!' Colin joked. He had come over from America to find out more about Guruji's practices, before returning home to start teaching them.

I noticed that Guruji always made sure that the children were included in the conversation at meal times. He turned to Rachel: 'Would you like to see a fairy?'

Her eyes lit up. Rachel was nine which seemed a good age for fairies – young enough still to be enchanted, but old enough to be impressed. She looked at the rest of us as if to ask permission before saying 'yes' to this impossible feat. We nodded enthusiastically. We were curious to know how he would play this game.

'I'd like that,' she said quietly.

'Do you have a special place where you think we might be able to see them?' Guruji asked.

'Yes I'll take you there. It's not far, just up the hill a little way.'

'Good. We'll go there tomorrow morning – just you and me. And tonight you'll come to the talk with us? You can sit beside me.'

Rachel seemed to grow taller in her seat. The thought of being asked to sit close to Guruji when all those people were coming to listen to him, naturally made her feel important.

'Do you think I'll be able to sit still long enough?' Rachel asked me on our way to the lecture hall.

'Of course you will. Don't worry, he'll look after you. He may not remember to ask you anyway.'

Guruji waited in the ante-room for everyone to assemble in the hall. Just like the first time I had seen him, he walked in jauntily and took his place on the raised platform in front of us. After a few minutes of meditation he looked around the room. 'Rachel my darling, where are you? I can't give this talk without your help. Come and sit here.' And up she went and sat by his side. He put his arm around her protectively.

Afterwards I asked her if it had been alright.

'I never wanted to move. Just once I saw his glass of water and felt like having a drink. But then he gave me some so it was fine.'

I concluded that our teacher seemed to know what he was doing.

To my relief Abigail had lost her voice for the few days that Guruji was there, but it seemed strange for her to be so quiet.

Colin and I took her up the fell to give her some attention and check on the water supply. I tried to explain what the problem was. 'I'm concerned that we might run out of water with so many people in the house. I need to check how full the tank is.'

'It's hard to believe that you get your water directly from the hill behind your house.'

'Oh we're still quite primitive here you know,' I teased.

'You certainly live in a beautiful place. I wouldn't have missed coming up here – it's been the best part of the trip.'

'I'm glad you think so. How are you going to start teaching when you get back to California?'

'With difficulty. The distances are so large. There are quite a few people who want to learn but it'll mean a lot of travelling. I'm the only teacher there as yet.' Colin seemed wise, gentle and self-contained. I doubted that he would have much trouble in getting volunteers to help him.

He lifted the slate from the top of the tank and I cleared a few worms and weeds out of the pipes and made sure that the water was flowing freely again. As we turned to go back to the house, we paused to look across to the Lake District hills. The first snows were dusting the tops and some delicate wisps of cloud decorated the sky.

'It's so clear you can see for miles. This place really is a little paradise,' I confirmed to myself.

'No doubt that's why we're all here.'

'Maybe it is . . . the magic of coincidence . . . '

And as we made our way down the hill, Colin took my hand to steady me.

Near the end of Guruji's stay, he asked me if he could see one of my poems. I knew that he had an interest in poetry and had written some himself when he was younger; but I suspected that his desire to see mine was a way of finding out more about me.

'I'll show you my poem about the evolution of the soul,' I smiled. 'You can check it for accuracy!'

'Tell me how it begins,' he asked with interest.

'With a speck of light . . . and it ends at the centre of the Universe. I'll fetch it.'

The next morning I met Guruji coming out of the kitchen. I was startled as I had not expected him to be there.

'I liked your poem,' he said, looking at me closely.

For a moment I stood transfixed. It was as though he was seeing through and beyond me, to a place that was neither in the past nor in the future. Perhaps it was only seconds that passed, but it seemed a while before he came back to focus on my physical form there in front of him. I looked at him more closely, drawn by the extraordinary depth of his dark eyes. All at once they seemed to fire up and sparkle and, in that instance, there was a moment of recognition. I realized that this man knew me better than I knew myself. Yet, in that knowledge, I did not feel afraid but strangely comforted. There was absolutely nothing that I had to hide from him.

'Usha . . . ' He whispered quietly.

'Usha?' I queried.

'It's your spiritual name. It means *dawn*.'

'Usha.' I repeated after him as if it were a new mantra. I was too overwhelmed to say more.

If love is the force of attraction, the divine energy that holds creation together, then why is it hounded by fear? Is it possible for a person to find a love that is free from pain?

The protective walls that we build around ourselves inhibit the flow of love. We create a grand array of games and devices to conceal our longings and fears and these become an impenetrable shield . . . the acts too polished and perfect. Until there is no need for them, we would never risk opening ourselves up to an experience of limitless love. That would mean that there was nothing between ourselves and another . . .

5

uruji showed Rachel her fairy. To our surprise he seemed to know that she had a book about them. 'Can you fetch it? I'll show you the fairy we're going to find.'

Rachel skipped off upstairs and returned with the book in hand and passed it to Guruji. After scanning through it quickly, he pointed to a picture of Rose-bay Willow-herb.

'This is your fairy,' he told her.

Rachel seemed surprised. Rose-bay was dressed in pink, had windswept hair, a secretive smile and her arms were opened up to the sky. She flew around among the petals on the flower heads.

'Read us the poem about her,' Guruji said softly.

Rachel recited Rose-bay's verse:

> *On the breeze my fluff is blown*
> *So my airy seeds are sown.*
> *Where the earth is burnt and sad*
> *I will come to make it glad.*
> *All forlorn and ruined places,*
> *All neglected empty spaces,*
> *I can cover – only think –*
> *With a mass of rosy pink.*
> *Burst then seed-pods, breezes blow,*
> *Far and wide my seeds shall go!*

We all applauded her.

'Now, shall we go and find her?' Guruji got up from his chair, took Rachel by the hand, and off they went.

Later that evening, when I was settling Rachel to bed, I asked about her time fairy-spotting. We were all curious to know what had gone on. They had both returned from their expedition looking very pleased with themselves.

'Well . . . I took Guruji up the fell to the place by the stream where we make our dens. He didn't get tired.' We had told her not to take him too far. 'We sat down together and looked at the picture of Rose-bay Willow-herb in the book. Then he asked me to close my eyes. We were very, very quiet. He whispered to me, "Now keep your eyes closed and look for your fairy inside your head – just wait and she'll come into your mind." And she did. I could see her clearly right there in front of me. So I just sat there watching her. Guruji was happy for me. Afterwards, when I'd opened my eyes, he told me that I could see the fairy whenever I wanted to. All I have to do is go up to my den, sit quietly with my eyes closed, and she will come to me.'

I was relieved by the lack of mystique. On hearing the story I realized that Guruji had simply given Rachel an appropriate visualization practice – and had not pretended that there were fairies dancing in the grass.

I realized that I would miss Guruji. Before he left England he told Walter that he wanted me to start teaching for him. 'That's ridiculous!' I retorted. 'What's the point of making me a teacher when I live up here?'

'That's what he wants,' I was told assuredly.

After thinking about the idea a while, I decided that I was pleased he had made such an impractical decision. It showed me that his prime concern was not in teaching vast numbers of people to meditate, but in giving us the individual attention and encouragement that we need. During his visit my trust in him had deepened.

The days shortened as winter drew in. I thought my parents would be pleased about my move north as, with sadness, they had seen the problems that I had faced during my time with Martin. I imagined that they would be relieved that I had at last found the courage to end the marriage and move away. And my father loved the limestone dales – he knew them well having often botanised there in the past. My removal to Dentdale, however, did nothing to comfort them. The remoteness of the place disturbed them. How would I ever find work, friends or another husband? These issues were high priorities in their eyes – in mine they had not figured. My freedom mattered more. But I did not want them worrying about me any more.

It was during the autumn that Rachel heard mention of the word 'divorce'. One evening I sensed that something was troubling her and that she needed to talk.

'Come here Rachel, are you feeling alright?' I wanted to encourage her.

She knelt down and put her head on my knee.

'Mum,' she said thoughtfully, 'please don't divorce Daddy.'

'Rachel, you haven't been worrying about that have you? It'll make no difference whether we divorce or not.'

'It will.' She spoke plaintively.

'Why should it?'

'It'll mean that you won't talk to him any more.' I was horrified by her misconception of the term 'divorce'.

'But that's not true.' I protested vigorously. 'Divorce is just a word – a piece of paper. It means what you want it to mean and nothing more. It's not going to change my relationship with Daddy. He'll go on coming to see us whenever he wants, and you can go and see him. All divorce means is that we are both free to go our own ways, and that's all. Please try and understand. I hate to see you upset about something that's not necessary.'

I watched her eyes. They seemed so full of sadness and longing. I drew her up to me and held her close in my arms. 'My darling . . . I promise you, nothing will change any of our relationships. You must trust me.'

When Rachel had gone upstairs I telephoned Martin. 'Call Rachel. She needs to know that you're there for her.'

He did so at once and I went to fetch her. 'Daddy's on the phone. He wants to know how we're coping in the snow.'

As she got out of bed, I saw that she had been crying. I was stunned. How could she have so misread the situation? How could I have misread her? I was determined that my children would not suffer silently, and for this reason I had always tried to be open with them. In this case, however, my attempt to bridge the gap between the adult and child worlds had not succeeded.

The evenings were long. The snows came and I was unprepared for their impact. Locals knew that they had to leave their cars at the end of the farm tracks when the forecast was bad, but I had not been warned. The roads were ploughed and gritted long before the farm tracks were passable. That year I could hardly believe the speed with which the dale was covered with inches of powdery snow so soon after it had begun to fall. The winds whipped up the surface flakes, spun them in the air, and dropped them at the backs of walls, in gullies and in dips. The drifts got deeper. For two weeks I had no choice but to make my way by foot between the banks of snow to fetch provisions from the village. A half mile of track to dig out was too big a feat for me alone.

Hemmed in by the surrounding fells, the severity of the weather and my own personal situation, it was hardly surprising that when I received an invitation to visit Colin in California in the spring, I decided to accept. Primarily he needed some help with teaching meditation, but he also promised a trip to Yosemite and a weekend's course on Lake Mead near Las Vegas. I would have to be prepared for three busy weeks over Easter. I had taken to Colin; he gave the appearance of being strong but gentle, and I looked forward to the chance of getting to know him better. Apparently he had a small business blending essential oils from natural fragrances that he ran from his home in Marin county just north of San Francisco.

By nature we all dream, and I had the tendency to believe that dreams can come true. The very thought that an unattached man had invited me to California filled my mind with romantic imaginings. In order to portray an image of self-sufficiency to my family and friends, I had tried to suppress my growing desire to have another relationship. Yet, inside, I was beginning to realize that they had probably been right: I was not going to last long without some male company around. Martin and I had finally gone our separate ways and he was now living with Susie. I was left alone with the children, my Dales house, and the knowledge that I had intentionally removed myself from a life of possibility. From that point on, Colin occupied much of my thinking time during those winter months.

It was for this reason that it seemed strange to meet him again in person. As I remembered he was soft spoken. 'Hiya Liza,' as he called me, 'Good to see you again.'

He reminded me of a cuddly bear. I was relieved that I felt comfortable with him again. 'So things are busy over here?'

Teaching was the only ground we had in common.

'Seem to be. I thought we could go down to the quay and have a meal to celebrate your arrival in San Francisco. Feeling up to it?'

'Of course.'

I had arrived in the early evening and, although I was not hungry after the flight, I welcomed the excuse to sit and be with my new companion for a while. I wanted to get used to him again. I was glad of the drive down to the waterfront and of the reminder that I had come to a thriving fishing port. Colin opted for an Italian restaurant with a view. Watching the lights on the masts swaying to and fro, and listening to the mesmeric sound of the water lapping around the boats in the harbour, I found myself drifting. I was deliciously tired. What a change this made from life in Dentdale. Colin began talking about plans for the trip and I was brought back from my reverie.

'I'm in the San Francisco choir and tomorrow we've got a rehearsal for the Carmina Burana. You can come along if you like.'

'It's powerful music; it'll get me in the mood for the trip.'

'Then the next day we're off to Yosemite – one of nature's masterpieces and not to be missed – especially for a lover of wild places like you.'

The first thing that struck me about San Francisco was its cleanliness, and then the size of its supermarkets selling an enviable selection of healthy foods, vegetables, fruit and juices. It was impossible to forget that one was in a sun-soaked, efficient, environmentally-aware modern city. The steep hills, the trams, the restaurants and inhabitants of every conceivable nationality helped give San Francisco a cosmopolitan flavour. I liked its liveliness and vision, and the fact that it seemed so different from England.

But there was little time to explore it properly before heading off for Yosemite. Our drive took us along never-ending roads and between orchards and wheat fields that reached as far as the eye could see. The only interruption to the vast expanse of space was the occasional dusty rambling farming town, with its brightly coloured hoardings to remind us that we were in real time. Everything was so big and open. At last, lit up by the setting sun, the outline of some hills appeared on the horizon.

'Is that the Sierra Nevada?'

'It is indeed. Are you glad to see some hills again? Just wait for Yosemite . . . '

When we reached the boundaries of the National Park, we began weaving our way through the thick lush pine forests, where the famed sequoias take their place proudly among the other native trees. A few miles further on we were greeted by the massive wall of El Capitan's sheer rock face towering impressively above us. It rose directly from the forest floor. A feeling of awe welled up inside me. No description could have prepared me for the sublime grandeur of what I saw. The contrasts of the scene – the gentle pines, the gleaming rock, the waterfalls that billowed out in wafts of foaming spay – moved me deeply. Slowly I let my eye explore the glaciated markings on the rock and the long column of water cascading downward from its source way up. I noticed that the pines became more stunted and contorted the higher up they grew, and then abruptly the tree line ended.

'It must still be cold up there,' I murmured.

Colin had arranged for us to stay in a log cabin. To be in Yosemite is to be absorbed into nature. To listen to the water singing its way along the rivers, to follow the streams and discover yet more waterfalls hidden away, to wander among the sweet smelling pine forests, was to experience an intimacy and depth with forces infinitely greater than oneself. It was a landscape that overwhelmed and inspired – the smells, the sounds and the sensual spirit of place.

'I want to breathe it all in . . . to explore it all.'

'You'll tire, eventually.'

And I did. In the afternoon of the second day we returned to the cabin weary from our day's excursion. The sun streamed through the windows and cast shadows across the room.

'Come here.' Colin motioned me to him.

'Why?' I asked nervously.

'Don't worry. I'm not going to hurt you.'

'I know. But I'm not sure what I think.'

'You don't have to think. Just be. Let yourself go.'

'I've been married a long time,' I spoke hesitantly, 'I've always been a one man woman. I don't know what I want from my life now. So much has changed so quickly.' I could feel myself withdrawing.

'Listen. Between men and women there are always undercurrents at play, like the eddies and flows in the river. Unsaid thoughts can be read, hidden feelings sensed and innuendoes understood. It's a natural process. And that's why there's nothing wrong with flirting a little. It's a part of the interaction, we do it all the time subconsciously. It's fun and alluring and provides us with the excitement and subtlety of life.' He tweaked my nose affectionately before going on. 'It's a way of communicating with each other that's all. But with you it's different. Since you arrived you've been distant, almost cold, as though you want to keep yourself hidden away. You're a lovely woman and not one of those slabs of rock out there. You need to open up some chinks in that armour of yours. Nothing's going to happen that you don't want – believe me.'

He was right: I was withheld. In a way I felt relieved that he had seen through my act and his insight attracted me more to him. I had spent many years cultivating the illusion that I was in charge of my life. But, as I stood there on the wooden floor, bare foot with my jumper draped around my waist, I felt peculiarly shy. Here in this beautiful place I was being asked to undress, to dismantle some of my outer walls of protection. I was not sure whether I trusted him enough for that.

'Come here.' He took me by the hand and led me to the bed. 'Just lie down with me a little while. I won't touch you.'

No doubt he had planned it this way. Bringing me to this place where I felt cushioned and protected by the splendour that surrounded me . . . offering me the security that I needed to give in, to give myself up. So much time had passed since the days of my youth when I had gadded around confidently. I was almost thirty and I felt inexperienced and naïve. It was as though I was a virgin again.

After we had made love, I lay back and stared at the ceiling. It had started to rain and the noise of the individual drops resounded loudly on the roof. It was a mournful, poignant sound. Suddenly an image of the heavens weeping came into my mind. Had I done wrong? Was I mistaken to break my resolve? I wanted to retain my individuality; I had waited so long and worked so hard for it. Now, unwittingly, I had allowed myself to be seduced and without knowing why, I feared the consequences. I closed my eyes but could not sleep.

Once away from Yosemite, our work began. After a few days of teaching on the west coast we flew out to Las Vegas and the desert. Not only was there a keen group of meditators there, but there were also others arriving from different places to be taught.

'It seems strange that this is a stronghold for meditation. They must need it.'

'The people who live here are very different from those who come to play.'

'I'd like to see the casinos . . . and have a go maybe.'

'In Las Vegas you have to pay for everything up front you know? No hotel owner will take any risks.'

That evening I had my taste of Las Vegas life: first a comedy show, then a meal out and finally on to the great gambling halls. As soon as I entered I was struck by the atmosphere. Tension hung heavy in the air but it was tinged with sad resignation rather than the excitement that I had expected. The number of machines was oppressive. I had expected more cards, roulette and green baize tables. After five minutes on a slot machine I was fifty cents up.

'That's it. I'm off.'

As I turned to go, I heard the harsh jangling sound of hundreds of dollar tokens spewing out of the machine next door to me. They came so fast that the player found it difficult to catch them. I looked at his face but he seemed unmoved, no doubt he was one of those caught in that never-ending spiral of loss and gain . . .

I was glad to drive out to Lake Mead for the meditation course. The desert was decorated with flowering cactus and I was back in the silence again. We rose before dawn, climbed a nearby dune, and sunk into deep meditation while the sun's rays spilled over the horizon. In the evening we sat by the lake, talking late into the night about the different routes that we had travelled to arrive at this point in our lives. It was a time of recollection and sharing. Since I had been in California, I had found the people easy, fun-loving and naturally interested in a way that I had rarely come across amongst people back home. Increasingly I felt drawn to life on this side of the Atlantic, not just because of the people, but because it was a land of such contrasts – the vibrancy of the cities and the compelling silence of wilderness like this.

Colin had been kind and had looked after me well. Nearing the end of my trip we mulled over our time together and contemplated the future. Colin seemed to deliberate over his words. 'I respect the way you bring up your children.' His comment took me by surprise.

'What makes you say that?'

'American children run wild. We get used to it, but whenever I'm in England I always notice the way you raise your children. I think *you* do a particularly good job.'

For some reason compliments embarrassed me and I steered the conversation in a different direction. 'I had Rachel when I was young so my life has always been restricted by children. But I've never regretted it. They've brought me a lot of pleasure.'

'Look,' Colin spoke quietly and took my hand, 'I want you to think about this carefully. While you've been staying I've been wondering if you would ever consider coming to live over here? We get on well together and we have the teaching in common – I can't manage the work load by myself. Above all, I think you're a beautiful woman and I like your children. I would enjoy having them around. For me it would be a ready made family.' Colin paused for a moment as though thoughts were chasing him from the past. 'Don't say anything now but when you get home think about it. I don't believe you should be tucked away among those northern hills. I'm coming to England again in June. Perhaps we could escape to a Scottish island together for a few days?'

'Escape' was the operative word. I had spent so much of my life escaping: from the academic environment of my childhood, from school, from the confused messages of my marriage, from my own body, from my own mind . . . always in search of more – more happiness and greater fulfilment. Would I find it in California? Taking risks did not worry me now. I had already risked and survived. The ease and openness of the Californian lifestyle, the sunshine and the warmth, the spectacular range of landscapes all drew me. As for Colin, he was protective and caring, had a wide range of interests, and was prepared to accept the children and me into his home. I recognized that this was a serious commitment for anyone to consider. Abigail was still young and Rachel would soon be embarking on the difficult teenage years. His offer was tempting.

When I returned to England I talked to Martin. He took a rational view: 'If you do decide that you want to go, I won't stop you . . . but I'll miss the children. I realize that you have to find a life for yourself now. Besides, I think you should know that Susie and I are going to get married.'

Whether it was the thought of his impending marriage that spurred me on, I was not sure. He obviously had no intention of preventing me from going and, since I was taking his children out of the country, he had every right to stop me. It seemed that the decision was mine.

When action takes over, the mind has less time to ponder and whirl. I realized that it was only by selling the house that I would have sufficient funds to fly the three of us to the States. Without a house I would have no place to store my furniture. I did not leave time for sentimentality to creep in. I put the house on the market and asked a dealer to come and value the mahogany tall boy, the oak chest and corner cupboard that my grandmother had left me. I arranged for some of the smaller, more valuable items to be shipped to California. The rest of my belongings I gave to my sister and some friends. Despite the fact that Rachel had settled happily in Dent, I told her stories about California that made it seem irresistible. She prepared herself for another change and explained the move to Abigail, even though she was still too young to understand.

Colin did visit England in June and we arranged to spend ten days on the Scottish island of Islay. While we were there he made a comment about my appearance which surprised me and prompted thought. 'Maybe you could lose a few pounds?'

'Lose weight?' I was aghast.

'Then you'd have a perfect figure.'

'Do you realize that you're talking to an anorexic?'

'I thought you were over that now.'

'I think you should accept me as I am,' I remarked in a surprised tone.

The house sold more quickly than I had anticipated, presumably because I had put it on the market for exactly the price that I had paid for it. I could see little point in prolonging the wait in order to make a profit. The decision to go had been made and it was best that I went quickly. I was off to a new life with different challenges. I began to break the news to the villagers whom I had got to know during the year.

'We'll miss you, Eliza. Are you sure you're doing the right thing? It's a hell of a long way to go for a fella.'

I walked up the hill behind Woman's Land to have one last look at the dale. I found myself beside the stream where Rachel had seen her fairy, and it was there that reality hit home. What on earth had I done? I let go some deep cries of anguish as if to rid myself of this bad dream. I wanted to encircle the house so that I would be able to remember it . . . so that it would be imprinted on my mind forever. But the feelings inside began to hurt so much that I became frightened. I tried to walk on further but kept stumbling because the tears were choking me. The pain got so strong that my body felt constricted and I found it difficult to breath. I screwed up my eyes to try and make out the house as it was situated in the valley. I loved it here so much. Why was I tearing it all apart? What had made me determine to change my life yet again? Only a year ago I had discovered this magical, secretive dale and now I was abandoning it to alter my life's course yet again. Martin was bereft at losing the children, my parents had finally despaired of me, I was distraught, and it was all too late . . .

Martin came to see us off. I felt ashamed at what I had done. As I escaped to the cloakroom to wash the tears away, I saw a sunken, ashen face in the mirror and I hastily put on some make-up for the sake of the children.

'It'll be alright when you get there,' Martin consoled. He knew me too well for me to hide from him. 'Just don't give him all your money that's all.' I was amused by his advice and managed a thin smile.

Under my breath I murmured, 'I'll miss you', meaning all that was familiar to me – my home, my family, my independence. As Martin hugged the children I could see him fighting back the tears. How could I do this to him . . . to them? I was taking his children half way round the world on a pipe-dream . . .

I knew before I went that Colin's house was too small for all of us, but he had said that he was going to build Rachel a little cabin in the garden that she could call her own.

'That's nice for you,' I comforted her. 'A little house all for you.'
'I don't want to be out here. I want to be near you.'
'You're very near us. I promise I'll hear if you call.'
The morning after we arrived, Colin suggested that I take the

children out for an hour or two so that he could get on with some work. The house was remote and I was unsure of where to find a play area. I decided to look for some shops instead. It was Abigail's second birthday in a few days time and I wanted to find her a present; but it seemed there were no shops nearby either, and I felt unable to ask for the loan of Colin's car so soon after we had arrived. Later that day I asked him if he would take us present hunting.

'Yes. I'll take you when I have time.'

I felt trapped: it was becoming all too familiar an experience. At that point Abigail's birthday became the main focus of my life. All I wanted to do was to make it happy for her. I wanted a cake, a party, an outing . . . anything. It was the first birthday that she was able to appreciate and Rachel would enjoy it too. The following day Colin was still busy. I pottered about arranging the few things around the house that we had brought with us, and wondered where the rest of our belongings would go when they arrived off the ship. Distance was rapidly growing between Colin and me.

It was obvious that Colin had realized that he had over-reached himself by taking us all on. His way of coping was by making himself into a Tolstoyan figure, who headed the household and took control. And it seemed that I had no choice but to allow this to happen. What else could I do? The situation was starting to feel reminiscent of the years I had spent with Martin. Had this great move to California put me straight back into the position that I had spent years trying to get out of? Had my old need for love and security ingeniously reared its head again and ensnared me once more?

Abigail's birthday came and went. The day after it, Colin offered to take us to the beach for the afternoon. We settled ourselves on the sands with a picnic, towels and swimming things. It was a golden day and the sea sparkled in the sunshine.

'Rachel,' Colin said, 'there's a spade in the car if you want to fetch it. The boot's a bit awkward to open though.' And he proceeded to explain how to do it.

As she ran off he turned to me and said: 'She'll never be able to manage it.'

I was infuriated by his dismissive attitude and at once made up some excuse to follow Rachel. How could he possibly assume that she was incapable of opening the boot of his car? He did not know her well enough to make those assumptions. She was no fool – in fact she was a bright girl. In the distance I could see her moving from the catch inside the car door to the boot and back again. When I reached her I asked how she was managing.

'I can't make it work.'

'Here – let me have a go.'

I tried each key, catch and gadget but I had never bothered listening to Colin's explanation, and Rachel had forgotten the details. I stood back, bewildered at the situation that we found ourselves in, then looked across the roof of the car at Rachel. She had grown so pretty over the years: her fair hair fell about her tanned oval face and her blue eyes shone out in the sunlight. Unexpectedly she let go a dazzling smile that captivated me. I smiled back. She laughed – then I laughed. Before I knew it we had both collapsed into uncontrollable giggles on that glorious Californian beach with the sound of the surf pounding away in the background. It was as though tension that had been building up inside me all my life had exploded in a final release of energy. I felt exhilarated and unbelievably free.

'What shall we do?' I cried through my laughter.

'I don't know.'

'We don't have to stay,' I told her excitedly.

'Don't we?' Rachel looked so free and radiant.

'I'm not sure where we'll go though.'

'We can be gypsies Mum. I know that we'll be alright.'

'Do you think so?'

There is a wonderful faith that emanates from children that radiates and inspires. At that moment, with Rachel nearby, I had no fear for the future.

That evening when we returned to the house, Colin went straight out again saying that he would not be back until late. There was no point pretending any more: the strained atmosphere between us had become too obvious. He needed time to think, as I did too. At the very least I was blessed with a few precious hours alone. I rooted through the cupboards and found a bottle of sherry and some apple pie. Oh for the relief of comfort food and drink, I thought to myself as I uncorked the bottle. After one glassful I felt better, after the second I felt almost myself again, reassured that I could recapture my identity so quickly amidst all this turmoil. Never again, I promised myself, would I live my life in someone else's shadow.

Colin returned the following morning. He spoke practically and without emotion. 'I've arranged for you to stay with my friend Susie. She'll look after you as long as you need.'

I did not doubt that the situation was harder for him than for me. This was happening in his own environment, his work-place, and among his friends and colleagues . . . Rachel and I got our things together as quickly as possible saying little. There was no point in prolonging the drama with lame excuses and reasons. I liked Susie: she was a carefree, slightly hippyish girl who had worked for Colin for several years. At times I wondered why he had not taken up with her. The idea of staying with her delighted me – I looked forward to getting to know her better. When she arrived to collect us she flung her arms around us, gave us all a big hug, and told us that everything would be alright. At once she suggested that we took ourselves away to the Redwood forest to camp for a few days.

Among the tall trees in the silence of the forest we saw no one but each other for days on end. We walked, uncovered lurking wildlife among the vegetation on the forest floor, played hide-and-seek with the children, and cooled off in the streams in the middle of the day. At night I dreamed wildly in my tent with Abigail snuggled up close beside me. I was exhilarated by the notion that momentarily I had been released from all attachments – except for my children of course, but they were a part of me. Having no home and few belongings made the whole world seem more accessible. I could go anywhere . . . or even stay here. I was free to choose.

By taking time out it was easier to observe how my old patterns of behaviour recycled themselves. It was as though I was locked into their rhythm. My desire to be loved had yet again dictated the course of my actions. I could see myself playing the same games, being swept along by the same dreams, pursuing yet another man in order to get the love and attention that I craved. Was this the reason that I had come all the way to California – to find this out? Maybe it was only by travelling half way round the world that I was finally going to realize that happiness was never going to be found through another. I had imagined that sharing my life with someone who had similar interests would fulfil my desires. Making the passage through life alone could be a lonely business – it was more fun to have companionship. But reaching out for it had led me to retrace old steps, and now I was hopelessly stranded. The few belongings that I had were in a boat half-way across the Atlantic, and the children and I had no home.

Deep within the forest I sat and meditated. As I closed my eyes I drifted off to a place of such all-embracing peace that I knew that I had gone far beyond the turmoil of the conscious mind. My head spun slightly as I spiralled down. It was as though I was an embryo again, enveloped in a fragile shell that offered me complete security and love. No fear or pain could touch me there – nothing could hurt me. There was just an innate knowledge that all my needs would be fulfilled, that I was being looked after, and some guiding hand was leading me on to where I had to go. When I finally emerged from the forest I felt focused and calm. The world appeared changed.

The first thing I did was to telephone Martin sensing that he would be supportive in this situation – such dramas brought out the best in him. 'I'm coming home. Can you see if there are any houses for sale in Dent?'

Martin's reaction was one of delight and he offered me help in any way he could. Since we had parted, I sensed that Susie was now the recipient of his emotional outbursts, so I was free to relate to him on more neutral ground. I held no resentment against him for his behaviour in the past and this made our relationship easier. When I arrived in London, he met me at the airport and handed me details of a house in the middle of Dent village. Immediately I set off for the drive north, remembering the journey that I had made with my sister just a year and a half ago. I had arranged to look around the cottage the following day with a builder and surveyor, assessing the repairs needed and gauging the feel of the property. These old houses were always in need of attention and could be adapted for modern living in many ways. But, from the moment I walked in, I never doubted that it was home. The estate agents told me that the owners were Quakers who wanted the house to be used by a family rather than it go as a holiday home. Apparently they had stood by their principles for several months. I made an offer and it was accepted. It seemed that the house had been waiting for us.

My first night back in Dent demanded celebration. I lit the new stove, bought a bottle of red wine, and the children and I sat on orange boxes and ate fresh eggs from the farm, bread and cheese. Margaret, who delivered our milk and had become a good friend, was amazed to see us back.

'What are you doing back Liza? You've been a heck of a long way round to move just two miles down the dale.'

'It didn't work out.'

'How long did it last then?'

'Six days.'

'Six days!' We both burst out laughing. 'Watch out now, there'll be someone else just around the corner you wait and see . . . '

'I think I need a break.' I felt wonderfully happy to be back in Dent – and this time I was right in the heart of the village.

With no furniture and little money, making the house habitable was an uphill task. Friends helped me by screwing planks of wood together to make bed bases, and I stained the wooden floors so I could manage without carpets. I scoured the markets for a pine table and some chairs for the kitchen. For the rest of our furnishings we made do with rugs and cushions. There was little I could do about the need for a damp-proof course, woodworm treatment, or the rotten window frames that needed replacing. I sealed up the draughts as best I could with polythene and drawing pins, and I kept two open fires going with wood that I collected from the river banks. A proper overhaul of the house would have to wait.

Once I had achieved a measure of comfort, I decided to go away for a weekend to brush up my teaching skills. I was drawn to the idea of starting up some meditation classes in Dent as a way of getting more involved with the local community. I also needed a break to realign myself. Going away on a course, even a short one, was like touching base – an opportunity to evaluate progress and look at the challenges that I needed to confront next.

It was during one of the afternoon seminars that I noticed Hugh. For some reason he seemed out of context there, but I was unsure why. He was tall, thin and appeared very English. It did not surprise me when I heard that he was reading Sanskrit at Oxford. I liked his slightly gauche manner, the openness of his smile and his wide-eyed innocent expression. There was an obvious attraction between us. Perhaps I should have held back in view of what had just happened to me but, since my time with Colin, my aloofness had gone and quietly, subtly, Hugh and I were drawn closer to one another.

Without restraint I found myself reaching out towards another man, another relationship, another question mark in my life. But Hugh was different. I had been dragged down deep enough to realize that any relationship based on need and an unequal flow of energy could never bring fulfilment to either person. There had to be free exchange between two people – a complete sharing. Hugh was younger than me, and in him I saw a quality of gentleness and openness that I had not experienced before in a man. He displayed none of the usual airs that were used to impress and flaunt. It was his tenderness that I fell in love with, his ability to love.

I went to stay with him in Oxford and he came to stay in Dent. We would go for long rambling walks, both in the meadows by the Thames and up the fells in the Dales. We talked tirelessly about the occurrence of coincidence, different life patterns, and of what the outcome of our fleeting love might be. We knew from the beginning that it was fated, that it was not to be . . . and within that knowledge I felt a lurking fear, for I did not want our love to end. It was a relationship of treasured moments, of an innate knowledge that we were not meant for one another, but that we were being offered this time together as a sacred gift. Sometimes, when love-making, Hugh whispered, 'Don't move . . . come without moving.'

'But I want to move.'

'Just let yourself come with feeling.' And I did.

I had never known that it was possible to have such a flow of living and loving, neither one separate from the other. To be able to open up to another without any restrictions and inhibitions getting in the way, was a new and liberating experience for me. Within the security of each other's love, barriers came down and the love just increased and intensified.

Yet, at the same time, tremors of my underlying fear were gathering strength. Knowing that this love was bound to end, the potential for one of us to get hurt became inevitable. Hugh was still young. He had talked of adventure and going off and exploring the world, while I was at a point in my life when I needed to establish a solid base. Within that knowledge lay my confusion. Why were love and pain so closely interlinked? They seemed to belong to each other in an endless cycle of being drawn together and torn apart again.

I realized that for me love was still an exchange . . . a bargain. I wanted Hugh's tenderness but I did not want the risk of being hurt. I feared him leaving me and I knew that it was bound to happen sooner or later . . . Meanwhile I clung to our love which, like a warm summer breeze, caressed and consoled. We lingered over meals that we had created together, we sat on the fellside or by flowing streams and let our imaginations wander off to different planes of existence, we stared at the sky and made pictures with the clouds . . . we touched, we stroked – it was a time of being totally absorbed by nature and each other.

'Catch the winged seed that spirals off on the wind,' he said reaching out his hand.

'Too late – it's gone . . . as you'll go sometime.'

'We have to live in the moment.'

'I can't.' And I looked away to hide my tears.

'Try,' he said touching my cheek fondly. 'We'll never forget this time together.'

I sat up abruptly: I could not take any more. 'Hugh, this has to end. Now.'

And so it was that I decided it was safer to inflict the pain myself, rather than to leave myself open to the possibility of getting hurt later.

'What do you mean?' he asked in astonishment.

I watched with horror as his initial look of surprise turned to anguish – an anguish that I knew so well. I spoke plainly in order to conceal my true feelings.

'Hugh, it's time you went and found your own life and I have to concentrate on finding mine. It's better that you move on quickly before we get more involved. Believe me, I'm sorry . . . I don't want to do this to you, but I just can't bear the thought of being hurt again myself. It's over Hugh – it has to be.'

I knew that the break had to be sharp. We had been too close for a ragged end.

'I don't understand.' I watched his eyes contort with emotion. 'Why are you deliberately breaking apart something that is so precious to us both? There's no sense in it. How often do you find something in life that is this beautiful? Why are you bent on destroying it?'

'Because it *is* beautiful Hugh. Please try and understand.'

I could not say any more. I did not want to watch him suffer – the pain of loss was too familiar to me and I cared for him too much. If there were to be a love that was boundless and free, surely there was no place for fear?

Through Hugh I realized that I had to get rid of mine.

When a spark ignites between two people, the experience can permeate every cell of the body and prompt deeper searching. It is difficult to interpret the feeling that is generated for it is beyond words. There is just the knowledge that some reservoir of indefinable energy has been opened up and, because of the circuit that has been created between them, it is allowed to flow. The energy is not explicable, but it is there to be drawn on . . . if there is the courage to do so.

6

'There is no death,' said Guruji, 'it is the passing through a door from one room to another.' Guruji was giving a course in England and he had just received a telegram saying that his own master, Swami Pavitrananda, had died in India. Guruji spoke softly. 'Light some candles. We'll burn them tonight and throughout tomorrow as a reminder that his light lives on. The course will proceed as usual and we'll begin with *satsang* tonight.' *Satsang* was the name given to the time when we all came together for either a talk or questions.

During the following days we asked Guruji about his relationship with his own spiritual master. He told the story of how he had first met Pavitrananda, of the stern but careful guidance his master had given him to bring him to a state of enlightenment, of the instruction he had given Guruji to live an ordinary life, and then how he had had to give up all his business activities, so that he could teach others to find spiritual fulfilment through the householder path. It was on the same course that Guruji suggested a new meditation practice for us.

'While I am in meditation, I want you just to sit and gaze at me effortlessly. It will be a way of allowing you to be in direct touch with Divinity, with that One consciousness from which we have all come and to which we will all return. I want you all to have this experience. The meditation will be a kind of communion practice. Whatever feeling or emotion you find welling up inside you, just allow yourselves to experience and release it. It will be a way of helping you to free yourselves.'

We washed and dressed up for the practice, believing it to be a unique occasion. I sat cross-legged on a cushion in the front row glad to have a good view of Guruji. When we were all settled, Guruji closed his eyes and began to meditate. The room became very quiet and the first thing I noticed was how still, almost stone-like, Guruji's face became. It was as though he had disappeared from his body. There was no flinch or flicker, no inkling that a person was inside the physical frame in front of me. I watched, intrigued by his apparent state of lifelessness, when unexpectedly his face began to change. It became malleable, like molten flesh that was capable of assuming different forms. At first I saw a gentle man with oriental features who seemed to embody wisdom, then all at once the mouth became an ugly leer and the face was old and grotesque. Momentarily I was disturbed by how this could be an aspect of Divinity, but then I realized that these were all impressions that lay in my own mind. I had no time to wonder more as the face dissolved again and re-formed itself as the image of a handsome black-haired youth whose smile enticed and allured. I thought of Martin and wanted the image to change again, so that I could have a glimpse of something more sublime. But all at once it returned to being the face of a statue, untouched by worldly worries or woes – a state of no emotion.

Never once did I divert my gaze, so transfixed was I by the form in front of me. The face began to pulsate, subtly moving backwards and forwards, vibrating in a golden glow and occasionally disappearing into the surrounding light. It was as though this face had come from Light to live a thousand lives.

Unexpectedly the sound of laughter came from behind me. At first it startled me, but then it made me smile. It sounded like tinkling bells that played up and down the scale, going on and on and on. Someone else began to laugh, then another, and from somewhere way across the room came the sound of crying. Amidst these tears and smiles, I remained quite still and calm, feeling only the smile on my face broaden, but not break. Eventually Guruji emerged from meditation and wiped a tear away from his eye.

As I looked around me, my glance met someone else's and my

gaze became locked into theirs. Entranced, I found myself unable to turn away. It was as though I was being swallowed up by them, my own consciousness was melting into theirs. There was no separation, no barriers dividing us. I was away from my mind – all analysis and judgment had gone. In that apparent state of emptiness, two people were merging into one another – both uniting in that One, all-embracing consciousness.

Gradually people got up, stretched and began to move around, smiling at each other and talking about their experiences. I felt as though I was waking from a dream.

From such experiences of mergence and the Divine, I returned home to confront the problem of my own personal management. I sank low. A cloud of depression that seemed to have no reason for being there, began to overwhelm me. Like a weighty blanket it sat on top of me. What alarmed me most was not knowing when it would lift . . . indeed wondering whether it would ever lift. Whilst I realized that a profound meditative experience could unleash deep feelings of negativity, I desperately sought a more specific reason for my state – but I could find none. I loved being back in Dent in my new house and, although I had no car and little money, my domestic situation did not worry me. The children made wonderful companions and there were plenty of household tasks to keep me occupied. In the evenings I tried turning to pen and paper, in the hope that through writing I would get what was inside me out . . . but it was all to no avail. I went to bed knowing that the following morning I would awake to the same grey gloom. I could neither banish it, nor find a way of escaping from it.

By chance Robert, who had instructed me in the practice of meditation originally, asked if he could come and stay. Over the years we had become close friends and, as there was no romantic involvement between us, we were able to talk freely and objectively about all aspects of our lives. During the day he took me out to explore some of the remoter dales, stopping for a pub lunch of real ale and local cheeses, and returning home to play scrabble by the fire in the evening. Gradually some light came back into my life. It was as though by sharing my thoughts and feelings with another, I was relieved of their pressure: my load lifted. Within the embrace of companionship and loving support, I was nurtured back to a state of stability and hope. Once again I felt at peace with myself, content to live alone with the children.

Rachel and I became more involved with life in the dale. She took part in the Christmas pantomime, while I became a member of both the local fell rescue team and the choir. I also ran some elementary yoga classes in the village hall, thinking that this might be a good way of introducing people to the idea of meditation. I was surprised by the number of people who attended. Once we had completed our yoga positions, we moved on to the pub where I joined in the local gossip and became more acquainted with community affairs.

I wanted to become increasingly absorbed by the hills and the life that went on in them. As spring turned into summer, I spent more time exploring the valley, observing the changes that each season brought to the hedgerows, meadows and the numerous gullies that were hidden among the fellsides. It was on a clear June day, on one of my bicycle rides up Deepdale, that I saw one of the instructors who worked at the Outdoor Centre in Dentdale walking towards me. I knew him through attending my classes in the village.

'Fancy seeing you here,' I called out.

His hair was wet and he had a towel slung over his shoulder. I was taken aback by our meeting, even though we were only a short distance from the place where he worked. I pushed my bike up the hill towards him noticing that it took me longer than usual to catch my breath. I acknowledged that this may have been more due to emotion than exertion. John had intrigued me for some time, but he had always appeared remote, both in everyday pleasantries and in conversation about his work. Now he was standing right here in front of me – wearing nothing but cut-off jeans and sandals, appearing so open and free.

He spoke enthusiastically. 'It's a beautiful day . . . I've just been for a swim. Why don't you go for one?'

'Where?'

'Black Dub. It's a deep pool further up the beck.'

'Is it difficult to find?'

'Just follow the road and you'll see a track off to the right. The pool is down amongst some trees as soon as you reach the beck. It doesn't get much sun, that's the only thing.'

'Why's it called Black Dub?'

'Slaves used to be brought to Dent from Liverpool and some escaped and intermixed locally. One fell in love with a village girl, but he knew that it would come to nothing because of local prejudice . . . so he drowned himself there in despair. Hence Black Dub. Whatever its history, it's a good place to cool off.'

Our conversation oriented around caves and caving, the activity in which the Outdoor Centre specialized. I expressed a wish to see what secrets these fells and dales held beneath ground.

'I've got a day off tomorrow. I'll take you to Ibbeth Peril Cave if you like. It's in the bed of the main river. It's a bit of a tight squeeze at the entrance but it soon opens out into a large cavern. Once in the main chamber there's a waterfall, some nice formations and a nicely shaped passageway off to one side. It's a good cave for beginners.'

'I'd like to go . . . ' I hesitated a little, 'but tomorrow I'm tied up with children. Sometime though . . . ' Momentarily I was torn between duties at home and the desire for adventure. I decided that I had better go quickly before temptation got the better of me. 'I'll see you around.'

When I got home I felt pleased that I had followed the line of duty. For me it had been a clear choice between my head and my heart, and I knew that it was time that I became more responsible. A nice-looking man, who lived locally, had just asked me to share an adventure and I had had the strength to say 'no'. My refusal gave me more confidence in myself, even though it was to be another six months before I was to have another opportunity of going caving. One thing I had learned over the years was that by chasing dreams, one often chases them away.

As autumn came and another winter approached, I wandered out onto the cobbled streets late one night to put out the milk bottles out and look at the stars. Dentdale was a good place to see them. As I cast my eye around the heavens, I heard the footsteps of someone coming out of the pub. It was John.

'How are you?' I said quickly. I wanted to catch his attention.

'Not so bad. It's a good night for stars.'

'Yes it is.'

He seemed slightly despondent and I was prompted to make a suggestion. 'Do you want some coffee before you walk back?'

He did not conceal his shyness. He made a couple of turns in the street as if to give himself more time to think about the invitation before saying casually, 'Alright then.'

For two hours we sat across the kitchen table and talked of his recent trips abroad, the daunting experiences he had gone through while out on cave rescues, his work at the Outdoor Centre and his thoughts about the future. I discovered that he had been at Oxford University, had initially worked as a research chemist, before deciding to take a few months off to go caving and travelling in Spain. When he returned he was offered a temporary job at the Outdoor Centre in Dentdale. Four years later he was bemused to find himself still here . . . still feeling that it was time to move on. Perhaps this explained his despondency?

'It's late,' he said suddenly looking at his watch. 'I'd better be getting back. Thanks for the coffee.'

'It's a pleasure. You still owe me that caving trip by the way.'

'So I do.' As he opened the door a blast of cold air blew in. 'Brrr . . it's cold out there.'

'Do you want to borrow a scarf?' As I handed him my long, brown woollen scarf, I imagined that it would be a way of drawing him back to the house . . . and to me. I had enjoyed his company.

'I'd be glad of it. See you then.' And off he went into the night.

It was over a week before John brought the scarf back.

'It's been useful. I had to spend several hours waiting around on the fell in a bitter wind checking to see if some students could locate some obscure cave. I was glad to have it.'

I sensed that John would never make a move. He would not have liked to intrude, to presume that I was interested. I realized that he was no emotional risk-taker, even though he might have been one physically. I could sympathize with his hesitancy. John seemed so gentle, so vulnerable, and I felt that that he could easily be hurt. He knew very little about my background except for the village gossip, which oriented around me coming from the film and theatre world. How could he possibly know that I was drawn to him because of his sense of ordinariness, his straightforwardness, his love of nature and the outdoors? He would only know if I told him.

If I were to embark upon another relationship I knew that it had to be right; I could not afford to make any more mistakes. I searched for the truth within myself. Had I at last reached a point in my life when I had enough emotional stability not to let my desires run wild in search of self-gratification? I believed that I had. I felt that my feet were more firmly placed on the ground – which was why I felt it was permissible to ask John if he would accompany me to the fell rescue dinner.

'You'll probably know more people there than me. I don't want to go by myself.'

'I'd like to come . . . if you're sure that's alright with you.'

'I'm sure.' And I smiled to encourage him.

When he let go, I was captivated by his openness and innocence. Through his smile he radiated a warmth and sensitivity that I wanted to touch and melt into. It seemed that I had been watching this solitary man from afar for so long. Now he was here, so close, seemingly willing to go for more interaction . . . more play. Like a child I was excited, filled with anticipation. All I had to do was to open my arms and let my distant dream become a reality.

As we sat on cushions in front of the fire drinking hot chocolate and talking about others who had been there at the dinner, John reached out to take my hand. He held it firmly and then gave a slight squeeze, as if to say that he was there for me if I wanted him. I noted that his shyness had gone. I fingered his face tentatively, enjoying his clear weathered skin, his vivid blue-grey eyes that shone out in the firelight, the tousled fair hair and his lips that broke into that bewitching smile. As I touched him he drew me closer and I let my head nestle into his neck. I loved his smell. It was of the outdoors and the earth, of human nature, of my father when I snuggled up close when I was young. Yes . . . for me John emanated those feelings of home, a home that at last I could return to. It was there for the taking. I suddenly became emotional and was aware of tightness in my throat.

'Are you alright?' He whispered.

'Yes, so happy.'

'Shall I stay tonight?'

'As long as I don't have to . . . '

'Shhh.' He stopped me gently. 'You don't have to do anything for me. I'll just stay so that I can be close to you.'

I felt outpourings of love for him. I needed to know that he wanted me for my own sake – not for my body, the odd night out, a bit of company on a cold night, or a place to drop off when he felt like it. I wanted to trust him completely, so that I could open myself up without letting my past fears get in the way.

I realized that I had never really trusted Colin. How clearly I could now see the ulterior motives that had brought us together. He had wanted a family, and I had wanted to be looked after. With Hugh it was different: I had trusted his love but not the constancy of our relationship. From the beginning I had known that we were at different points in our lives and I had become frightened by the inevitable outcome of our parting. Unless that element of trust was embedded into a relationship from the beginning, how could there ever be complete openness between two people?

John wrapped his arms around me and held me tight. All I wanted was to be absorbed by him, taken deep within . . . As we lay by the fire in the sitting room caressing one another, it was not an offering of our bodies that became important, but an offering of the innermost core of our beings. Without physically making love, we explored a deeper level of union and became one in our embrace. Instead of being pulled by the pangs of need and desire, we were raised to the heights of a love that was free and ecstatic – an experience that was liberating and not binding. After a lifetime of being swallowed up by my emotions, and lost in the struggle of seeking a way out – that element of freedom mattered above all else.

John came the following evening after work. He often finished late as there had to be some evening supervision for the students who attended the courses. I made him a hot drink, heard about his day and he listened to mine. Within that trust that we had experienced the previous night, it seemed so natural for us to undress and go to bed together. It was as though we had known each other for years. After that night, it was rare for John not to come down after work. As the snows came we heard that the villagers had noticed footprints leaving the house early each morning. They were pleased. There was nothing they liked more than a good story with a happy ending.

It was the ordinariness and honesty of John that appealed – his lack of airs and graces, his ability to enjoy life for itself without the need for an endless search for meaning. He had no desire to impress or to influence. He was one of those rare people who is able to express themselves freely without fear of what others may think. As far as he was concerned there was no point in playing games. He liked to be straight. He had the skill of cutting through superfluity and getting to the bare essentials. It was his direct approach to life that intrigued me. Not only was it expressed in his attitude to life, but also in his feelings towards me. Unashamedly he rejoiced in them. Unabashed he celebrated our love with whoever else was around. And when we were alone together, he would look into my eyes intently, before kissing me with a passion and tenderness that I had not known before. In so doing he breathed new life into me.

He was easily absorbed into the household, no questions were asked or fuss made. Like Rachel, John had joined the local drama group and this gave them a shared interest. He also had an instinctive ability to make the outdoors fun for children. I knew that through John, both the children and I would be able to develop a closer connection to the land. I wanted to understand it as he did, both above ground and beneath it. He knew about weather patterns, hydrology, different cave systems and life on the fells. He had an intimacy with the landscape that I envied and admired. After being out on the hills, or underground in the caves, he would return home flushed and invigorated by the day's experience.

'I'll teach you to master the skills of single rope techniques.' John was keen for me to learn. 'It's an easy way of descending hundreds of feet down a shaft. Mind, you have to be fit enough to climb back out again but, since you're clipped to a rope, you can rest whenever you like. It's much harder work on ladders.'

'I'd like to learn.'

'At the Outdoor Centre there are some trees that are rigged up with platforms fifty feet high. We can practise ascents and descents there. On my next day off we'll have a go.'

'That won't be much of a day off for you.'

'With you it's different . . . everything's different. Let's take Rachel too.'

As he guided us through the techniques of how to use the appropriate bits of ironmongery to go up and down, he congratulated us on how quickly we learned.

'You'll be going straight down the three-hundred-feet shaft of Gaping Gill before long.'

'No thanks. But I'd like to see it sometime.'

'A lot of people find the trees difficult to cope with as you can see how high up you are. Underground it's dark, and you descend into an abyss.'

Through John I entered another world. He belonged to these hills. He had been coming to the Dales to cave, walk and climb since he was a child. Beneath ground he became like an animal who could assume different forms, according to whether he was faced with a narrow passage, a boulder collapse, a waterfall or a traverse. In the caves he was at home: on the fells he roamed free. Nature was his solace and the closer he interacted with it, the more exhilarated he became. He breathed, lived and loved the great outdoors and the more time we spent together, the more confidently I followed him to greater depths and heights. He introduced me to a different world, that was not only tangible and accessible, but which also held within it the capacity for excitement and aesthetic appreciation. To John anything else was an enigma and best left so. The hills and caves were his source of inspiration.

From those first nights together we never spent much time apart. Our decision to marry was not meant as a distinctive threshold in our lives, but merely as a means of celebrating our togetherness with our families, friends and the local people. Everyone was delighted with our news. John's parents were pleased that he had found a partner who was willing to settle in Dent; and mine expressed their utter relief that at last at the age of thirty-one I had met a sensible man who, they hoped, would influence me to live a more rational, ordered life. We filled the village hall with a memorable mix of people that included our families, outdoor enthusiasts, meditating friends, locals and farmers, and we danced the night away to a ceilidh band. The following morning we put our bicycles on the train, and watched while the landscape changed from the hills and dales of the north into the wild and rocky seascapes of Cornwall.

We stayed at the holiday home where I had spent so much time as a child. While there, I came to a decision about my future. Having just returned from an invigorating day out, clambering down into hidden coves and sea caves that I had not seen before, I broached a subject that was close to my heart. 'John – I've decided that I'm not going to teach meditation any more. I'm not going to meditate either.'

'Why on earth not? It's not for my sake I hope.'

'I don't think so.'

'Then what is it?'

'I know that you're sceptical about the spiritual part of my life . . . but that doesn't bother me. Actually I quite like your cynicism – I find it strangely refreshing. But when I meditate, I know that you're wondering where I go to in my mind. The truth is that I don't go anywhere in particular. I just return to a place of sanctuary, a cosy nest of comfort and peace. But I have you now.

I don't want anything to come between us – to interrupt our sense of togetherness. I don't ever want you to feel that my meditations are taking me away from you. That's not the point of them. You mean far more to me now than any belief system or meditative experience.' I paused to gather my thoughts. 'So I reckon that the answer to your question is 'no'. I'm not doing this for you. I'm doing this for me – because of my feelings for you. They come before everything else.'

'I'm very touched.' I could tell that John was moved by what I had said.

I continued: 'But I wouldn't do it if you asked me to. If you had, I'd be clinging on for dear life to some sense of identity. It's the fact that you ask nothing of me that enables me to give myself to you. From now on, you come first in my life.'

'I wouldn't like you to think that you had to change yourself for me. I love you too much for that.' As he spoke he ran his fingers through my hair, slid them down my face and touched my lips.

I took his hand and looked at him intently. 'Giving myself to you is not giving myself *up* to you. There's a big difference. I always want to feel free with you . . . to be completely open. I want to be able to say what I think without any fear or restriction getting in the way. I never want to feel imprisoned in a relationship again.'

'I don't want that either. And there's no need for it.' John got up and stretched. 'We should always say what we want and right now, I want a glass of cider.' As he got the flagon down from the shelf I could see him smiling to himself. My earnestness always amused him.

I went to squeeze him from behind. 'I'll join you in one . . . '

'I don't think we'll both fit in!'

And that is John – from the sublime to the banal in two seconds. It is his art.

Our time together brought us both gentle pastimes and daring adventures. Neither of us had much money nor means of transport so, when John was free from duties, we would often spend the days domestically. In the autumn we went gathering rosehips by the riverbank or clambered up the gills in search of the ripest rowans, so we could mush them and make then into wine. Conscientiously we kept up with the odd house repair and regularly collected wood for the fires. We took turns to bake the weekly batch of bread, created elaborate bean and lentil stews, and made jams and marmalades from the fruit in season. Despite the fact that we had to conserve our resources, for us life was a celebration and we lived well.

When we were able to borrow the Outdoor Centre's van, John showed me different cave systems. Once I had mastered the technique of abseiling, it gave us more flexibility to plummet deeper shafts, and push into the remoter reaches of the hundreds of miles of cave that riddle the Yorkshire Dales. The landscape contrasted so markedly with anything above ground that, through exploring the caves, it felt as though I was discovering a new form of art.

The sculpted shapes of the passage ways, the intricate scalloping on the rock, drew me to touch . . . to feel its crevices, its durability, and wonder at the effects of water and time on something that appeared so solid. I was intrigued by the sense that a cave is essentially a combination of darkness and nothingness. It is a hole – an empty space that has been created by thousands of years of erosion – which contains such beauty. All we see is the shape that is left behind when nature has worked its miracle.

I found the business of getting into the caving gear cumbersome. After one trip I had shivered with cold to such an extent that my concentration and hand movements had begun to fail me. As a result we had spent some money on buying me a warm padded suit that I wore underneath a plastic oversuit. On top of that I had a harness, various bits of rope and gadgetry, and Wellington boots that had a good grip.

As soon as we entered a cave, I felt invigorated by the echoing sounds of rushing water, the smell of earthiness, the taste of vibrant air as it wafted through the clean passage ways. Continually I found it a struggle to contort my body into the different positions needed in order to move through the cave. But the physical aspect of the trip challenged me in way that I had not experienced before. Manoeuvring a bag of rope, spare lights, and myself over rocks and boulders, along narrow slits, across traverses and up waterfalls, tested the strength and flexibility of my muscles to the limit. But as I descended a hundred-foot shaft with a waterfall cascading down beside me, all the tension dissolved as I was left awe-struck at the spectacle that surrounded me.

'Hola-a-a,' I shouted as I launched myself off the ledge and slid down the rope into the blackness. I gazed around me in admiration at how the cave changed from a narrow slit into a vast gaping hole. It seemed to take no time at all before the ground came up to meet me and I landed with a bounce off the rope.

'Rope free.' I called up to John when I had unclipped myself.

Standing well back, I watched his tiny light bobbing around at the top of the pitch before he too swung free to make his descent. As he took me to different grottoes, I became ever more entranced by their beauty. 'I want to hold this in my mind.' I said again and again. What seemed like a myriad glistening white straw stalactites hung from the ceiling.

'It's impossible to describe it, isn't it? You can see why I wanted you to see it for yourself.'

'I can.'

As we moved through the active streamways, pushing our way against the force of the water, the scenery changed from elliptical passages to canyon-like gorges. Occasionally we would pause to study a particular group of formations, or peer into a side grotto, but something kept us going, drawn along by the sensation that there was always more that lay ahead unseen. Eventually it was sheer physical exhaustion that made us head back for the surface, the knowledge that we still had all that way to climb up and out. When we emerged like moles into the light, we were dazzled by the brightness. Squinting and smiling, we de-rigged ourselves and wearily headed back home. As I sank into a deep hot bath, I experienced a physical and emotional exhaustion that was uniquely satisfying. What I had seen was sculpture in its purest form.

The times I felt fear were not at the top of a hundred-foot pitch, but when John was called out on a rescue. Too many of his friends had died, either underground or on the crags, for me to feel sanguine about putting himself in danger. I shuddered at the thought of losing him to a rock fall, a flash flood, or another person's mistake on a pitch. The late night call-out, John hurriedly getting his gear together, a brief description of the cave, him disappearing off into the night . . . and me left to wait. While lying alone in bed, my imagination could wander free. I had heard too many stories about searches in dubious places for lost cavers, casualties that had been recovered after falling scores of feet, dead bodies that needed retrieving after a boulder collapse.

'You'd want everyone out if I was in trouble,' was John's familiar refrain.

That was true. I would.

Usually it was not until it was getting light that I would hear the door go, the rucksack dumped on the kitchen floor and the kettle put on the stove. A wet, mud-splashed, tired caver stood in front me, either elated by success or smitten by the thought of the casualty who could not be saved. As I touched his face it felt so cold. 'Scrambled eggs or bed?' I would ask as a way of taking his mind off his ordeal.

'Eggs first, then bed,' he replied while pouring the water out of his boots. Then he would murmur: 'I'm so lucky . . . so lucky to have you.'

A long and difficult rescue provided a salutary reminder of everything we had together – the children, our home together, and the love that we had between us.

The birth of Charlotte temporarily interrupted our caving exploits. This time, with antibodies increasing in my blood owing to my rhesus negative status, I knew that my third baby was bound to need a spell in intensive care. I was less well prepared for the fact that I would be stranded in a hospital twenty miles away from Dent – and we still had no car that John could use for visiting. The situation prompted us to think again about transport. When Charlotte's condition had stabilized and we were back home, we heard about an old camper van that a friend was wanting to sell off quickly. To tempt us, he offered to include a whole-plate photographic enlarger – the deal was clinched.

As John was involved in running cave photography courses as part of his work, he was delighted at the thought of being able to further his hobby without relying on the Centre's equipment. He had long wanted to capture the underground world on camera, but to do so was not easy. Not only did it mean taking cameras, tripod and flash guns into a hostile environment, but the setting up of a photograph needed the help of a compliant assistant. The thought of painting the caves with light, however, appealed to the theatrical part of my nature – and I was excited by the challenge of encapsulating their magic within a frame. I decided to offer John my support.

How long it seemed since I had revealed the patterns of light and shade on film. Alongside my growing love for the Dales landscape, I had also developed a high regard for the people who lived and worked among the hills. Many of them had become close friends and I wanted a way of demonstrating my empathy with it all. I now understood the importance of giving creative expression to inner passions lest they turn in on themselves. John's enthusiasm, the new enlarger, access to a darkroom, and my own need for self-expression, all encouraged me once more to look at the world through a lens.

As the hills folded into one another and retreated into the distance, mist cushioned the tops and temporarily concealed any dividing line between land and sky. As wisps of cloud drifted apart, a finger of light pointed out the gentle gradients of the fellside, the dips where gullies hid and becks cascaded down. From moment to moment an isolated farmhouse, then a cluster of trees, a limestone outcrop would be picked out, only to be quickly shrouded again in thin haze. I wanted to envelop myself in the transience of the scene. There was nothing permanent about this place. To work with light is to have a glimpse of an ephemeral, ethereal aspect of existence.

Through a large-format camera, I noted how different types of cloud interrupted the sunlight and cast varying patterns on the land. The fell-tops and dales could be affected in a myriad ways. Either I focused on the wide open landscape or on detail – frosted leaves, mist rising from the river, water swirling over a smooth rock, or a lone geranium clinging to a wall. The camera opened my eyes to a subtler world of movement and light – fleeting moments of nowness – in which a scene is frozen and I was transformed. In fractions of a second I was privileged to experience unique moments in nature.

John and I inspired each other to penetrate deeper within the landscape, to create more dramatic effects underground, to venture into more extreme conditions, so that we were able to convey how the hills affected those who lived and worked among them. Together we tried out different film and developer combinations, assorted printing papers and experimented with technique, so that we could achieve greater depth and tonal range. We visited galleries and scanned photographic books in search of inspiration and knowledge. Essentially we taught ourselves to tell the story of a place that we had both fallen in love with independently.

'Na then, what do ye want me doing?' Asked a farmer who had worked among sheep all his life.

'How about sitting on the barn steps?'

'As though I'm having a crack, like? I don't normally have time to sit about . . . only when you come clicking.'

'Come on . . . how about having your dog in the picture?'

'Now you're talking. I'd like a good picture of Shep.'

The gentle banter allowed me time to gauge how I could best portray a character, and decide what light would be most appropriate to enhance the well-worn features. Written into a person's face is their life experience, both the hardship endured and the good times enjoyed. I set myself the task of conveying raw mood, of revealing the effects of time, weather and lifestyle on humankind. In these people it showed so well. As I looked through the camera and observed the subtleties of information, an intimacy developed between the sitter and me. I became absorbed in them . . . lost in their presence. A woman with her pinafore blowing in the wind, a shepherd grasping his crook, a child milking a goat, lambs suckling, a cow calving – each became an intimate study of life in the dale.

As we collected together pictures of the landscape, the caves, and Dales people throughout the year, we became aware that a unique story was emerging. It was a new angle, a broadened vision of the northern hills that was being revealed. My father, who had spent his working life in publishing, was beginning to visit us more regularly. Now that I was settled, he realized that he had a reliable base from which he could pursue his passion for botany. But he was also drawn to our life in Dent. The days he spent with us were precious to us all, for at last we had the opportunity of getting to know each other on a more equal footing. In the evenings, after a day out on the limestone crags recording his sedges, we would linger over a meal, savouring our elderberry wine with a selection of local cheeses. The mellower we became, the more ideas flowed as to what publishing opportunities there might be for us.

We agreed that we would have a greater chance of success if we approached a local firm. Before long we had managed to arrange a meeting with the manager of a printing firm a few miles away. Not only did this printer have an interest in producing quality books, but he also believed that the way of life in the hills should be recorded for posterity. On both counts we answered his dream. Within weeks a bond was formed that was to last for many years. John and I were the photographers and authors, my father acted as editor and advisor, while Colin became our publisher and friend.

In the pub directly across the road from our house, we celebrated the launch of our first book with our families, friends, and as many of the local people as space allowed. Everyone was thrilled to see themselves in print for the first time, and the party went on from midday until late into the night. John and I felt proud at being able to offer the Dales people a fresh look at the place in which they lived and loved so dearly; and I was received, not just into the heart of the community, but back into the bosom of my own family. It was a time of reunion. Despite all my past adventures it was generally accepted that, six years into my second marriage, I had come home at last. I had a loving husband, children who brought me great pleasure, and a means of self-expression that everyone could enjoy. It was an achievement that no one could have foreseen a little while ago.

'But what do you mean by subtle energy?' John probed.

'It can't be seen, or proved. You can't contain it in a test-tube, for it's the test-tube itself. I'm talking about an energy that underlies all existence. It's just there. Another name for it is Divinity or Grace.'

'It's not there if you can't prove it. The subtlest form of energy that's known about is . . .' And John would launch into an explanation about sub-atomic particles and quarks.

Our conversations about the meaning of life always ended abruptly. They were broken apart by the seemingly unbridgeable gulf that lay between John's scientific mind and my own mystical vision of the Universe. Occasionally I yearned for a conversation about the purpose of life, reincarnation, karmic patterns and so on, but for five years I had remained silent. During that time I had chosen to devote myself to John; and, in so doing, I recognized that I had achieved a level of human love that I had never thought possible.

'Love. That's it John. You can't prove love but you can't deny that it exists. It's the energy that flows between us, that connects all existence and binds people together. Love is the subtle energy that I'm talking about.'

John went quiet. We were both lying in bed together, staring at the ceiling, and searching for answers inside our heads. Despite all that we had together, I was beginning to realize that I had kept a part of myself repressed during our marriage. Every now and again I could feel it well up inside and demand my attention.

'John.'

'Yes.'

'You know that you mean more to me than anything else . . . apart from the children of course?'

'You don't have to say that. You've shown me that in so many ways.'

'Maybe it seems selfish to say this, but occasionally I feel I need something more. At times I feel lost, as though I need guidance. I know that on the surface it appears that I have everything – including the experience of human love that eludes so many. I should be so happy . . . yet there is something that cries out inside me. It's the same cry that I had when I was a child . . . when I was searching for love and I could not find it. That search has taken me through so many strange adventures until eventually I found you. Yet even now there is still a desire to have something more, to have more exalted experiences of love. I don't want you to feel hurt by what I say. I just want to resolve some questions that have been haunting me throughout my life. Do you understand that?'

'What will you do?'

'I don't know. Maybe by opening myself up to the problem, an answer will come.'

Meanwhile John opened himself up to challenges of his own. He always hesitated before telling me about potential caving expeditions abroad. Although we had little money to fund them, I always encouraged him to go as I recognized the importance of his pushing the boundaries of his own caving experience. After all, that was how he gained his inspiration. Yet he remained torn between his sense of loyalty to us, and his desire to pursue his own personal interests. This time he had heard through the Centre about an expedition to explore one of the deepest known caves in the world: it was situated in southern France. The trip would take days of preparation and to reach the bottom would mean hours of continuous caving with the possibility of sleeping underground. But, on this occasion, John accepted the invitation without hesitation.

'Try and take some pictures of it if you can.' I was aware of the problems involved in carrying the extra equipment.

'Apparently there are some beautifully decorated parts of the cave.'

'Will you manage the cameras and tripod all the way down there?'

'I'll try.'

'The Berger.' I repeated the name of the cave. 'You really want to go to the bottom don't you?'

'It's an opportunity of a lifetime.'

With rucksacks packed with thousands of metres of rope, karabiners, spare tackle, lights as well as the camera gear and warm clothes, John boarded the bus along with friends, colleagues and several members of the cave rescue team. A sense of nervous anticipation prevailed as the final bag was squeezed into the last corner of space.

'Take care. Don't push yourself too far. I want you back in one piece.'

'You're not the only one. I'll miss you.'

'You won't when you're there,' I smiled knowingly. 'Goodbye my love . . . goodbye. I love you.'

'I love you too.'

I returned home to a phone call from my mother.

'Why don't you to come to Scotland with us? Faith is having one of her large house parties. She would love you to come and it will be something different for the children. We can walk and swim, while your father fishes and botanises.'

Rachel had just turned eighteen, and had gone to stay on a kibbutz in Israel for three months before beginning her training in a Lancaster hospital to become a nurse. Abigail was eleven and Charlotte six, and they were delighted at the thought of us having an adventure of our own. We agreed to go.

But, little did I envisage that a genteel family holiday of a kind that I had not known for years, was to be the start of a spiritual adventure in which I would come face to face with the mystery of the Self. All I had to be was open to the answers . . . but was I yet open enough?

It can take years before we truly understand the relevance or value of a particular event in our lives. At the time we are too immersed in the situation, confused by its detail, overwhelmed by accompanying emotion, to be able to stand back and get a clear view. It is only when we have moved from the role of actor to spectator, that the scene falls into place in the jigsaw puzzle of our lives. Time is needed before we can see how individual circumstances make up the final story.

Meanwhile we stumble along in the dark, convincing ourselves that we are moving towards the light.

7

There was a strange assortment of people at Ardtornish House. Retired dons, keen botanists and gardeners, fly-fishermen, an ex-dean and Rootie, the endearing ninety-year-old cook, were some of those who made up the party. Abigail, Charlotte and I provided the younger element. Throw a diverse mixture of people together and it is not difficult to find adventure.

An invitation from an elderly gentleman with failing eyesight to go for a trip in his leaky boat, becomes difficult to refuse for fear he might take offence. But there lay the excitement as I tried to get hold of the helm for sufficient time to ensure that we were never too far from the shore. Other times I would escape with the children into unknown terrain, only to get lost on our return among acres of thick, tangled rhododendron bushes that enabled us to imagine we were in deepest jungle. Charlotte cried as I became more disoriented, but the irksome crawl out on our stomachs made a good story to tell during the long summer evenings. More serious drama occurred when the cook's only son died. On hearing the news I offered my condolences and then took the children off for a swim in a nearby loch so that the retired dean could be left in peace to counsel and console.

It was with him that a connection was made. Hardly a word had been spoken yet, when our eyes met, a knowingness was there that created a magnetic pull between us. One evening I found myself sitting next to him and I was drawn to open a sensitive subject.

'I feel lost. I'm not sure in what direction I should be going.'

With a distant look in his eyes, his voice seemed to come from another time, another place . . . I even wondered whether it was him that spoke.

'I think you should be teaching meditation again.'

I nodded thoughtfully; I wanted to thank him but I was too absorbed. Initiated by his words, a chord resonated somewhere deep inside.

As we drove back through Glencoe, a thin line of mist threaded its way beneath the line of peaks. Its scalloped edge made it seem as though it was cradling the mountain tops. The wild valley was momentarily turned into a fairyland and I allowed the image to imprint itself firmly on my mind. The ethereal beauty of the scene offered hope for the future.

John returned home elated by his success down the Berger. I arrived back bitten by the desire to renew my spiritual quest. But where, or to whom should I turn for help? I acknowledged my need for guidance – I had done enough groping around in the dark on my own. But no conventional religion or belief system drew me now. I was a universalist, accepting that all different paths ultimately lead to the same end. What I wanted to do was to speed up my own process of unfoldment and for that to happen I needed some spiritual prodding. Not only did I want to understand the nature of my Real Self, but I wanted to experience It too. If True Reality lay beyond the material world, then I wanted to transcend earthly attachments and desires so that I could reach It. Once again, my endless yearning to be free was reasserting itself.

I reviewed my life's search. I had starved myself in order to find a deeper, truer meaning to life; but by doing so I had nearly left the world altogether. I had learned to meditate and discovered that we all belonged to one unifying consciousness, but that understanding had only succeeded in satisfying the mind. It had been the practice of meditation itself that had given me access to that reservoir of inner silence that helped the creative impulse to flow. And, with Guruji's guidance, I had found the courage to stand on my own and open myself up to deeper experiences of love, exploring its potential through the realm of personal relationships. Yet, if love were limitless, surely it was more than the entwining of two separate parts? Had it not been my endless search for love in its many and varying forms that had ultimately acted as the magnet in leading me on?

Guruji was the only spiritual teacher whose compassion and wisdom I had never doubted and always trusted. But I did not know what had happened to him? Over the years I had heard that quite a few of the meditators had left the movement in order to find their own path. I was hardly surprised as the unique aspect of Guruji's teaching was to help individuals draw upon their inner strength, so that they could find their own direction. In the process people were bound to go off on their own track, as I had done on mine . . . for a while. How different Guruji was to those teachers who sought to influence and persuade.

I decided to begin searching through my old telephone directories in the hope of finding a contact. Eventually I managed to track down a teacher who lived in the north. 'Hello,' I said hesitantly, remembering that when I gave up teaching meditation for Maharishi, it had been intimated that I would never be welcomed back into the movement. But of course, Guruji's teaching was so different. 'Tony, is that you? It's Usha.' It seemed strange to use the name Usha again after all these years.

'Usha! What a wonderful surprise. How are you? It's good to hear you again.'

There was a warmth in Tony's voice that made me feel glad that I had called. He proceeded to regale me with stories about the time I had trained him as a teacher, and how he had slept on our kitchen floor when the house had been brimming with visitors. I had always remembered him as being someone who was fun-loving and kind. Eventually I managed to bring him back to the point. 'I was just wondering about Guruji . . . does he still come to this country?'

'He's just been here. In fact you might just catch him before he flies back to South Africa. Try phoning Rajesh and Jasmini at this

London number. And make sure you keep in touch this time.'

Immediately I did as Tony suggested and a woman answered the phone whom I presumed to be Jasmini. 'Who is it? Usha? Oh yes I've heard about you. Unfortunately Guruji has just left for the airport – but I'll be talking to him when he arrives in Capetown. Do you want me to give him a message?'

'Just tell him that Usha's back.' I knew that there was no need to say more.

It was a few days later when a woman from Ireland telephoned to say that Guruji wanted me to call him. As I dialled the code for South Africa I felt nervous. How would he respond to me after all this time?

'Hello? Guruji speaking. How can I help?'

As soon as I heard his deep, resonant voice at the other end of the phone, all feelings of apprehension disappeared. 'Guruji – it's Usha.'

'Usha . . Usha, I have been calling for you to come back. What has taken you so long?' His voice was gentle but had extraordinary power, and the waves of love that radiated down the phone filled me with a sense of joy and relief. 'I have been waiting for you Usha, I have been waiting for so long. I need you . . . I need you as a centre for my teachings. Could you come to South Africa for a while? I would like to teach you some special meditation practices. Think about it. Listen to the talks that you have missed while you've been away. I write a lot of poetry now . . . and I also paint. I'll write you a poem, Usha. You've never been far away from me . . . you know that, don't you? Give my love to John and the children and write to me soon. I want to hear all your news. You mean so much to me, Usha . . . so much. '

I put the phone down and looked across at John. 'The power and intensity in his voice . . . they were overwhelming. I feel as though I can't move.'

'What did he say?'

'That he's been calling for me to come back.'

'I thought I'd been hearing something.'

'What? Oh John . . . ' I dived onto the sofa and grabbed hold of him. 'Don't tease. Spirituality is a serious business you know!'

Empowered and exhilarated by the phone call, we both collapsed with laughter. I needed that release.

Guruji had visited Dentdale for a second time during the early days of my relationship with John. They had got on well, and Guruji had asked us then if we had thought of marrying. Over the years I had occasionally wondered whether he had realized that it had been my marriage to John that had taken me away from both him and meditation. There lay the paradox: with Guruji's help I had found the strength to go off on my own . . . and Guruji *wanted* to lose us if it meant that we found ourselves. As he had always said, the role of an outer guru is simply to awaken the inner one – the spiritual path is about realizing our *own* potential. Spirituality is wholeness . . . the living of our life to the full. It is the direct experience of the divine force that underlies all existence.

How different this philosophy was from so many religions and cults. More often than not, these are held together by a set of rigid and narrow beliefs which can result in limiting both vision and experience. If consciousness remains restricted, how can we possibly open ourselves to the totality of Love, or give ourselves freely to one another? I had heard Guruji say that there should be as many religions as there are individuals on this planet, for everyone unfolds in their own particular way. I could not envisage how such an all-embracing philosophy could ever be held together within an organized structure. As far as Guruji was concerned, whatever could be done to help a person progress along the path, must come first. For centuries religions had fallen prey to placing rules and dogma before personal spiritual unfoldment. The mystics came to remind us of more permanent truths.

Over a period of several weeks, I listened to all the talks that Guruji had given in England during the years that I had been away. I became aware of a change in his teaching. In the early years he had explained in detail such concepts as karma, Grace, reincarnation, the passage of the soul, *samskaric* impressions, various aspects of yoga and so on. But, as time had gone by, he had started to probe deeper into the realms of individual experience, urging people on to have the courage to let go of their conditionings and open themselves up to their Inner Self. I also realized that Guruji was getting weaker. I had heard that spiritual teachers were often sickly people, for the more powerfully the spiritual force is channelled through them, the less significant their body becomes. Not only did Guruji suffer from a weak heart, but he was also now diabetic. After each tour away from home, his wife had to spend several weeks nursing him back to good health.

It was early in 1987 that Guruji telephoned me from London, where he was breaking his journey over a weekend as he flew from Canada back to South Africa. He was staying with Rajesh and Jasmini.

'Usha, I know it is a long way from the north, but is there any chance that you could come and see me?'

'Today?'

'Yes. Jasmini says that you can stay here overnight.'

'I'll do my best.'

I was excited at the prospect of seeing him again after so long. John found out the train times while I packed an overnight bag. Later that afternoon I arrived in London and made my way to the house as directed. Jasmini, an elegant Jamaican woman, answered the door and gave me a warm welcome. She then explained that Guruji was resting. I felt quietly relieved as it gave me time to get to know my hosts, hear news of old friends, look at recent photographs of Guruji with his family, and generally begin to feel as though I belonged once more.

It was an hour or so before I heard the noise of shuffling outside in the corridor. I was not sure what to expect. I had been writing to Guruji since I had made contact again, expressing my desire to progress faster along the spiritual path. I had told him that I wanted not only to discover the nature of my Real Self, but also to experience It directly. I was tired of my old habit patterns holding me back – all those fears and needs that had suffocated me for so long. I wanted to throw off my inhibitions, let go of my desires, and open myself up to the power of Grace, which I saw as being synonymous with the ultimate experience of Love. I realized that it was not going to be easy. The scriptures said that it was a path for heroes and that courage was needed, yet I had never really understood why. No doubt Guruji would show me. That is what I had come back for.

I got up from my chair expectantly and peered around the corner of the sitting-room door. Guruji was standing at the bottom of the stairs in his pyjamas and dressing gown. He was wearing spectacles and had hooked his walking stick over his arm so that he could light a cigarette. I smiled to myself at this vision of a spiritual teacher. I had come back to have illusions shattered and habits broken, and I acknowledged to myself that he had got off to a good start. After all, he had always said that he was no pedestal guru and did not want to be treated differently from anyone else. He was certainly not trying to impress me. All at once he gave the warm welcome that I had expected for myself to a young Irish meditator, Anu, who had just arrived. After expressing his delight in seeing her again, he eventually turned in my direction.

'I need to pee.'

I realized that the lavatory was through the kitchen and that he would have to pass by me as he walked through. I stepped out confidently to attract his attention and, without a word, he gave me a bear-like hug.

During the evening Guruji entertained us with Indian prayers, poems and games of charades. I had realized from listening to the tapes and talking to others, that he now taught through play rather than just by expounding philosophy. At supper I sat next to him and he began to pay me a little more attention.

'Have some chicken, Usha.'

I had not eaten meat for years, but something prevented me from interrupting the meal to explain that. I realized that biting through flesh would be difficult after all this time but, in the circumstances, I saw little option than to face the challenge. Over a period of time I had become an increasingly lazy vegetarian and recognized that I had not been feeding myself properly again. I had been getting tired, and sinister patches were appearing on my legs that the doctor thought might be due to protein deficiency. Only too aware of my previous eating problems, I reasoned that a little meat might do me good and decided to try it. To my surprise I enjoyed the chicken in its spicy cream sauce, and my vegetarian days were over. One pattern broken, I confirmed to myself. I felt better for the experience.

'Why have you been away so long, Usha?'

'I had to learn to walk on my own two feet.'

'But you've been going around in circles.'

'Maybe. But I had to find that out for myself.'

I was glad that I had no fear of answering him back. He seemed to summon an openness that I found it easy to respond to. After supper the games quietened down, and Guruji spent some time looking at our book of photographs of the Dales that I had brought for him.

'Some day we'll do a book together, Usha.'

'I'd like that.'

Guruji turned to Rajesh and Jasmini. 'I would like Usha to help me with these letters. I want her to learn how to go through them.'

Gradually the others drifted off to bed and I was left alone with Guruji. I read each letter out loud while Guruji listened carefully to the problems that the writer related. After I had finished each one Guruji would take the letter, place it on his knee, and put his hands over it.

'Now we will send some healing.'

We closed our eyes, brought the person to our mind, and radiated out to them positive healing thoughts. I was surprised at how profound and real the link seemed between the writer and me. The last letter was from someone suffering from cancer, which prompted Guruji to ask whether I thought there should be specific meditation practices given in such cases. I was touched that he not only sought my opinion, but then considered my response carefully. His own words came into my mind: 'True teaching is the sharing of oneself with another.'

It was not until the early hours that he put his work to one side and turned to look at me as he had done all that time ago in Dentdale, when he had given me my spiritual name. Once again he appeared to penetrate the surface layers of my being and transcend all form. This time I responded by looking directly into the depths of his eyes. I wanted to say something but I faltered on the words.

'I - I feel as though I have come home.' As I spoke I knew that I was voicing a desire and not a reality. In that instance, I realized that I still had a long way to travel. I could feel the separation that divided him from me, and knew that any experience of Oneness was but a distant dream.

'All the colours . . . they are so beautiful,' Guruji murmured as he gazed through me. 'I should have my paints to express them, but it is too late.'

Was he perceiving the subtler levels of my being – discovering how far along the path I had come? Was he exploring the dark areas that needed lightening and deciding how he could help me get rid of the dirt? That was why I had come back. My small self was like a muddied pane of glass and Guruji would have to serve as an abrasive if it were going to be cleansed quickly. The light of the True Self had to be able to shine through. Yes. Of course the process was bound to hurt . . . and that no doubt was why courage was needed.

The following morning Guruji asked Anu and me to pack for him. I liked the fact that he trusted us to sort through his belongings. I noticed in his brief case that he carried the Saint Francis prayer: '*Lord make me an instrument of your peace, where there is hatred let me sow love . . .* ' Yes, he too needed reminders, and I was reminded of his humility. Before he left for the airport, we gathered together in the sitting room.

'Usha, I am planning a trip to Cyprus with a few of the teachers from different countries. I would like you to come . . . Anu you too. I want to intensify your spiritual practices. I may not be around for much longer . . . ' His voice faded. 'It is important that we spend as much time as we can together. Rajesh will let you have the details. We are thinking of going just before the spring course in England.'

'I'll try and be there,' I said confidently.

Anu and I waved him off and she then drove me to the station.

'Come to Cyprus and have a hard time!' Anu joked in her soft Irish accent. 'I made the mistake of buying him a scourer once. It was meant as a hint to say that I was ready for a bit of cleansing . . . boy, have I paid for it Usha.'

'Has it been worth it though?'

'Oh yes. It hurts while you're going through it – but he does it with so much love. Afterwards I always feel lighter and freer. Like you, I want to get rid of the junk that I've been carrying around for far too long.'

Anu had more recent experience of his ways than I did.

The cost of my airfare to Cyprus appeared in the form of an unexpected royalty cheque. This time it was John's turn to encourage me to go off on an adventure. When I arrived at London Airport I found that some of the American and Canadian teachers had just arrived: the plan was that we should all fly on to Cyprus together. I looked to see if there was anyone I knew from the past. To my delight I saw Roopa – a teacher from California.

She greeted me warmly: 'How great to see you again Usha. Do you remember me? I used to admire you from a distance in the old days.' Her dark curly hair accentuated the clarity of her skin, and her smile radiated a warmth and joyfulness that made me feel immediately at ease amongst this disparate group of people.

Now that there were twenty of us in the party, I hardly expected any special attention from Guruji; so I was surprised when he drew me off to one side.

'Usha, I'm glad that you have come.'

'I'm pleased to be here.'

'I just want to tell you that there may be jealousies while we are away. But remember – I love you and I'm always with you.'

'I know that.'

'You're very special to me.' And he gave me a reassuring hug before rejoining the rest of the party.

I realized that the idea of us being together in Cyprus was so that Guruji could bring our attention to those patterns, or conditionings, that were causing the restrictions within us. I wondered at mine: I was all too aware of my incessant desire to be looked after and made to feel secure. These primal needs had motivated me through childhood, my relationship with Martin, and even during my time in the north. Yet, although I had now achieved a successful marriage and a means of self-expression, I knew that these same traits were still preventing me from feeling free within myself. Once again, I yearned to break out of all my restrictive boundaries, so that I could experience a fulfilment that transcended both life and art.

Apparently Guruji had fasted and done special practices in order to intensify the spiritual force that flowed through him; he wanted to be a powerful and effective channel to help us wash away the dirt. I was excited yet at the same time apprehensive. I did not know what to expect – none of us did. The only certainty was that we were bound to have to face parts of ourselves that we may have kept hidden for years.

A bus took us from the airport to the apartment block that had been rented for our stay. It had been arranged that Guruji would share a flat with Vidya, an American teacher who had assisted Guruji for many years, and her husband Sujay. Roopa was in the flat opposite with her partner Panu and Sutriya, another American teacher. I was on the floor below with Anu and the Irish contingent.

None of us had any idea what the programme would entail, indeed, whether there was to be one at all. The first afternoon, after we had settled in and bought some basic provisions, we gathered in the sitting-room of Guruji's apartment expecting to hear the schedule for the next ten days. He offered us none, but instead asked each of us to go up to him in turn. Either he held our heads or touched our feet, and it became clear that he was beginning to work with us in a different way.

'While we are here in Cyprus, you're going to shift a lot of dirt.'

Guruji spoke slowly, and his words had power and passion. I

felt my stomach tighten. Over the years he had become more challenging and had ceased to pull punches or skirt around sensitive areas. It was as though there were now no holds barred to the spiritual force that flowed through him. Among this group of teachers there was no need for him to measure himself. Those who had been around him for years had grown to understand his different ways of teaching. It was not always comfortable, but the benefits of being freed from the patterns that haunted our lives and inhibited self-expression, were there to be celebrated and enjoyed.

The following days merged into one long emotional upheaval, of an intensity that I had never known before. The *satsangs*, such as they were, took place at any time of the day or night, either in Guruji's bedroom or kitchen with us all crowding in to a small space. The informal atmosphere made it easier for us to be open to his teaching. Deep negative feelings were dredged to the surface in order that we should be made aware of their influence upon us. Yet, because of the continual flow of love that was transmitted through Guruji, it was as though we were all cushioned and supported throughout the process. Cyprus was termed a spiritual holiday. In actuality, for those who chose, it was a momentous opportunity for self-discovery. Some experiences were banal, others awesome, but always they were tailored to our individual needs.

I was squatting in a corner by the door watching Guruji explain to Chetan, a middle-aged gentleman, the technique used by Ramakrishna to release some constrictive energy in one of his closest disciples.

'For someone to achieve a state of enlightenment, it is the focused attitude of the student that matters – the preparing of the candle and the matches. Lighting the flame happens in a moment. When Vivekananda became enlightened, his master Ramakrishna made the final adjustment by pushing his disciple in the chest . . . like this.'

I watched on, amused by the scene that was taking place in front of me. Guruji raised his leg and placed it on Chetan's chest and gave it one short, sharp push and then another. Suddenly, without any indication or warning, I felt as if I had been shot through by a bolt of energy. Immediately I cried out, putting my arms over my head and curling myself up into a ball as a way of protecting myself from any further blast. The shock of the impact had been great and I hurt inside. A moment later I found myself collapsed on the floor sobbing quietly. All I could hear was Guruji's voice projected softly in my direction.

'Did you feel that, Usha?'

I raised my head to reply with a nod. There was nothing more I could say. I was in no state to ask for any explanation or meaning. Was that a release?

When powerful emotions overwhelmed us, we sought comfort in food, drink and each other. When Guruji was resting we would escape to a nearby restaurant, order some sumptuous meal and wash it down with lots of Aphrodite wine. On occasion we would go to a bar opposite and dance into the early hours as a way of getting rid of some tension. As the days went by, I could tell that feelings were becoming more charged. Any degree of equilibrium that we might have had on arrival was now being severely tested. And, as the process of release went on both around Guruji and through interaction with each other, there were times when I wanted to be quite alone.

One day, when I was feeling particularly vulnerable, I slipped away from Guruji's room to go back to my flat. Tempted by some sparkling wine that had been left in the fridge, I opened the bottle and savoured a glass – it was cool and refreshing. Whether it was the relief of having some time to myself or the effects of the wine I was not sure but, briefly, I managed to abstract myself from the drama that was going on and retreat into a quiet, still space inside. I felt deliciously at peace . . . for a short while . . . Whether it was the loud bang of the flat door, or the accusatory tone of the Irish teacher's voice that shocked me more, I was not sure. Whichever it was, I shuddered at the impact.

'Didn't you know that wine was meant for us to share?' She barked.

Quickly I tried to reassure her: 'Don't worry. There's plenty left. I can go and buy some more if it means that much to you.'

But she persisted in her accusatory tone. 'We could have had that as a celebration and you've taken it for yourself. How could you have been so selfish?'

It seemed that my retreat had unexpectedly become like a battlefield; I was on the receiving end of one blow after another. In my vulnerable state, I was unsure whether I was strong enough to take it. I stayed there for a while listening to her insults, but my eyes filled up and the lump in my throat got bigger. The last thing that I wanted was to give her the satisfaction of watching me break down in front of her. So, to avoid that humiliation, I headed for the door. I heard her voice ringing out behind me.

'Are you finding it difficult to cope?'

As I opened the door I saw Sujay standing there, looking relaxed in his jeans and sneakers and with a broad smile on his face.

'Hey, what's wrong Usha? I was just coming to ask you out for something to eat.' Touched by his kindness that seemed so contrary to everything I had just experienced, I collapsed in his arms. 'Come on now, what is it? Let's go – you can tell me about it over dinner.'

We sat across the table from each other and, as I related the incident, its absurdity became more ridiculous. We began to laugh.

Sujay consoled me. 'She's jealous of you Usha. You've come back after all those years away and Guruji gives you so much attention. The wine was just an excuse to get at you, that's all.'

'Do you think so?' I felt better for hearing his view.

'I'll tell you what. I'll take her a bottle of the finest champagne.'

Within minutes he had purchased a bottle from the waiter and was on his way back to the apartment. When he returned he was smiling.

'What did she say?' I asked intrigued.

'I didn't give her a chance to say anything – I just handed it to her with a smile. Usha, you know you don't have to put up with that sort of thing. There's nothing heroic about standing there and taking someone's abuse.'

'I know . . . you're right. Pretending to be brave and suffering inside is an old trait of mine that's been with me since childhood. It's time that I learned to stand in my own strength. If I did, presumably I wouldn't get so affected by what others say. It was such a relief to see you there . . . the welcome escape route. But I can't go on escaping forever.'

One afternoon, a little while into our stay, Guruji asked us each in turn how we were feeling. This time I tried to put my inner confusion into words.

'I'm being torn in two. I feel as if I've lived my whole life as half a person – cut off from my twin. It's as though I'm always searching for that missing part of myself. I'm lost and confused.' It seemed so difficult to express the sense of separateness that I so often felt.

'Usha, merge with me – into that One consciousness. There lies your answer.'

'If only I could . . . '

'You can. It's here and now . . . so near if only you knew.'

Sometimes when feelings became too explosive, I would escape to the sea and swim, or look for shells on the beach. But time away did not always succeed in re-establishing a state of calm. Irritated by my inability to cope, I would return to Guruji and demand his help. 'What do I do with this feeling? Tell me.'

'Don't fight it, Usha. Just let yourself experience it as a physical sensation and gradually it will lose its hold.'

I became aware of a burning feeling across my chest and began to observe it. I watched how it gripped me, constricted my lungs and made it difficult for me to breathe. It reminded me of the time I had walked up the fell to say goodbye to Woman's Land and I had choked on my grief. But this time it was different. The more aware I became of the pain, the more I found myself able to merge with it and, slowly and surely, it began to lessen its hold. When it eventually disappeared, a sense of calm washed through me again. Silently I offered my gratitude to Guruji. There had been no analysis, no questions, or delving into reasons. How different this seemed from the world of psychoanalysis. All Guruji had done was to give me the support and guidance that I needed to let go.

My deepest areas of vulnerability became more apparent as the days went by. In my desire to love and be loved, I could see that I often behaved deviously. I had done the same all through my life. I recognized my need to be valued, appreciated, respected and praised, but I also realized how I manipulated people and events to bring this about . . . even my show of courage could be perceived as a way of winning admiration from others. I was tired of being controlled by such deceptive games. It seemed as though I had spent my life chasing an illusory goal – when a desire remained unfulfilled I suffered, and that suffering would then in turn lead on to another desire. Liberation and Love – these were noble ideals but how were they to be achieved? Surely I had to let go of the incessant desire to be loved? Was that not the deepest, most powerful conditioning of all? It seemed that the only way out of this endless maze was to become so filled up with Love that there was no need to seek it from anyone else.

I wrote Guruji a note:
> *Please help me. I want to become more self-contained,*
> *Love Usha*

It was not long before Vidya came to fetch me. 'Guruji wants to see you.'

'Oh no . . . ' I cried out spontaneously. I sensed that I had invited some new ordeal.

'Come. He is insistent. It will be alright.'

I admired Vidya. She gave the appearance of being calm and efficient, even though I knew that she was finding it hard to cope with all the demands that were being put upon her. For many years she had not only acted as Guruji's carer while travelling, but she had also served as an exceptionally conscientious secretary. When she was going through a crisis of her own, she never forgot her duty as note-taker, recording every aspect of his teachings, whether he was giving a *satsang* or entertaining guests. She had a softness and gentleness about her disposition that endeared her to me, and contrasted with Sujay's more heroic, extrovert stance. He acted as her protector, coming to her need when he saw fit . . . as recently he had come to mine.

She took me to Guruji's room where Roopa, Sujay and one or two others were discussing different kinds of exotic fillings that they put in toasted sandwiches. Because of the light-hearted nature of the conversation, the atmosphere appeared relaxed and informal. After they had agreed on the best recipe and procedure, Guruji got to his feet. 'I want to show you something. I'm going to remove some veils of karma. Just sit and watch.'

None of us quite knew when Guruji was being serious or when he was playing around. We had all been caught out in our time. Over the years many meditators had left the movement, unable to cope with this particular aspect of his teaching. No one liked being shown up: it was humiliating to have one's defences exposed in public. But, since all of us had deliberately placed ourselves close to Guruji's fire and were only too aware of the consequences, there was a good-humoured feeling among us. We genuinely did not mind whether Guruji performed trick or treat.

First he placed his hands on Sujay's head. I was sitting next to him and was relieved that the attention was somewhere else. It was only later I realized that Guruji, in his masterful way, had placed me in the role of the relaxed observer. My mind was open – not gripped by anticipation or expectancy. Suddenly I saw Sujay fall back on the bed, and the next thing I knew was that I was crumpled up in a heap on the floor. Another blast of energy had seared through my body and brought me to my knees. The tears flowed from me in sobbing cries. I became disoriented as the room whirled around me and then, from somewhere above me, I felt Guruji's arms drawing me up to him as he whispered in my ear, 'Oh my darling Usha, come home . . . come home.'

I gazed up at the ceiling in my room. It was like coming round from an anaesthetic. I was cold and shivering, shaken by the momentous experience of what seemed like having my body ripped open. I did not want to stay there alone. I got up from my bed tentatively, pulled on a warm jumper, and went to look for Roopa.

'Usha are you alright?'

'No . . . no. I can't stop shivering.'

'Come here and snuggle up.'

I lay down beside her. Her motherly nature and form was just what I needed. She put her arm around me and held me tight. I nestled close to her, putting my head in the crook of her neck. I began to feel warmed through by her embrace. To me she was the essence of womanhood. At that moment she became my sister and mother rolled into one, offering me all the nurture and support that I could ever have wanted.

'What happened?' She asked softly.

'I've no idea.'

'Maybe we'll never understand what is happening here,' Roopa said thoughtfully.

'And maybe it doesn't matter that we do,' I concurred.

'All that matters is that we end up freer – so we can radiate more love.'

How simply, how beautifully, she had put Guruji's teaching into words.

As the days passed, it became clear that even amongst the devoted students who were there, some of us were less afraid of exposing ourselves to Guruji's fire than others. The energy that was radiating from him was so powerful that at times it terrified, as I had witnessed first hand. Some people preferred to escape to the mountains or visit the monasteries. I was one of those who chose to stay close so I could experience the full force of the heat that burned through him. For me there was no choice – it was like a magnet. One afternoon, when there were just a few of us about, Guruji called us to him.

'Come, I want to deepen your powers of communication.'

Roopa, Vidya, Sutriya, Anu and I were doing some clearing up. I felt as though I had known them for years owing to the extraordinary days that we had spent together. I had seen less of

Sutriya. She was a bright, independently-minded woman, whose training had been in psychiatry and who had no inhibitions about challenging Guruji. But he usually responded with a tease, telling her that it was mystics and not doctors who knew about the workings of the mind. Together we went into Guruji's room and, for the following hour or so, he put us through a combination of practices the relevance of which I did not understand at the time.

'Usha, hold one of my feet and Roopa, you hold the other.' He stretched out his legs on the bed. 'Now, let us close our eyes and meditate and, as we do so, I will empower the energy that flows between us.'

Each of us in turn performed this routine, first with him and then with each other. My face glowed red with the heat that was being generated in the room. I could sense subtle energy vibrating in the stillness of the room; it rebounded from the walls and seemed to hold me in a state of suspension. It was as though a link was being created between those of us in the room, that was far more profound than any ordinary form of communication. No words were necessary. I knew that what was happening was far beyond the mind.

'Now I will show you something else. Pull down the blinds, Usha. I want the light in the room to be dimmed. Now watch me. I am going to meditate and, when I do so, I will go into the body of Krishna. You will see.'

I could sense the internal questioning among us. I had always been glad of our mutual cynicism. Guruji had never encouraged blind acceptance. Any serious seeker who sought to rid themselves of their layers of conditioning had to ask questions and have doubts. Yet, because of the extraordinary atmosphere in the room, it seemed an inappropriate time for him to play games.

Guruji sat with his legs crossed at the top of the bed and closed his eyes. I watched him, enjoying the experience of sitting so close to him while he entered a state of *samadhi*. I allowed my eyes to relax so that they were not focused precisely on his form. After a little while, he appeared to come and go as I had remembered him doing during the meditation practice of communion. I found myself wondering whether he was an apparition or really there . . . for he began to retreat into a haze of light. I remembered Guruji telling us that we should try not to analyse experiences as, if we do, the mind becomes active and cannot settle. So I let myself drift and go deeper. As I did so Guruji's form began to melt away and a radiant, shimmering, blue-gold light shone out in its place. The colours were so vibrant that it was like nothing I had ever seen before. I sat mesmerized and enchanted by the sheer beauty of the vision in front of me and sank still deeper into meditation. Then, from within the light, I saw the distinctive smile of Krishna shining out. The image seemed real and tangible . . . was it possible to retreat into the Oneness and reappear in another form? Were there really no boundaries, no time or space? Was there just the One eternal moment of nowness?

Perhaps here, at last, was a glimpse of the Truth. How often had Guruji said that Krishna, Buddha and Christ were the greatest teachers that had ever walked this earth. How often had he explained that the greater the force of negativity in the world, the greater is the positive force that comes to restore the balance. That is the role of the mystic. The more power that can be generated within them, the more likely it is to ripple outward and cascade down the centuries.

As Guruji emerged from meditation, the image faded. Yes. I realized that it was all so close . . . just as he had said.

The next day I visited the old quarter of Limassol to wander through the back streets and remind myself that I was in an ancient middle-eastern town. I wanted to buy some presents for the children and get my life back into perspective again. The smell of bread wafted out of the open baking ovens and the markets overflowed with fresh herbs, fruits, dates and vegetables of every kind. I went to the castle and climbed the steps onto the roof so that I could get a better view. Across the sea was Palestine on whose fertile ground the message of Love had been imparted nearly two thousand years ago. Why did humankind stray so easily? Why was our small self so clever at leading us away from the Truth? I suddenly felt honoured to be in the company of a mystic and murmured a prayer of gratitude. When I got back to the apartment I found a bottle of wine on my bed with a letter of apology from the Irish teacher.

We arranged that we should take Guruji out for a meal to celebrate the end of our stay in Cyprus. He dressed in his white suit and Vidya and Sujay accompanied him across the road to the restaurant. It was never easy taking Guruji out socially, as his behaviour was always unpredictable. He often used such occasions as teaching situations. We had a long table to accommodate us and I found myself sitting across the table from Guruji. Glad to be close, but relieved that I was not responsible for looking after him, I wondered how the evening would unfold. The other tables began to fill up with a mixture of tourists and local people.

'Shall we say grace?' Guruji raised his voice slightly in order to get the attention of the whole table, and together we sang the universal Hindu prayer of peace. The waiters and other guests fell quiet, acknowledging that this was a sacred moment for us all to share. We opened our eyes and waited for Guruji to do the same, but he remained with his eyes closed for much longer than usual. Vidya looked at him first, and then at the waiters who were ready to serve our meal. She paused a few moments longer, and then took the initiative.

'You can start serving the meal,' she indicated to the waiter.

I admired her confidence and realized that she was obviously practised in handling such situations. Guruji remained in meditation while we helped ourselves to an assortment of side dishes. Gradually we came to the conclusion that he must have slipped into *samadhi*. Half way through our first course, with gentle nudges from Vidya, he emerged but refused to touch any food. Instead he put his hands together in the *namaste* position and bowed his head to us all. Vidya tried again to tempt him with some food but he ignored her efforts. Instead he looked across the table at me.

'Usha, will you take Sujay and tell all the guests in the restaurant how much I love them.'

'Really?' I was taken aback by the request. 'Do you think they'll want to know that?'

'Go now, Usha.'

I could have stayed in my seat – Guruji did not mind if we chose to ignore him. It was not for *his* sake but for *ours* that he asked us to do these things. Through such situations he was offering us an opportunity to find out more about ourselves – and that is what I was here for. I wanted to be challenged: I wanted to discover more about myself. I glanced across at Sujay who looked aghast at what we had been asked to do. I had a vision of him escaping, so I quickly went across to him to try and reassure him.

'Come on Sujay, we'll find a way of doing it tactfully. It'll be alright.'

'We'll end up in the police station.'

'It's only a lesson in not minding what others think.'

'We'll get thrown out. There's a time and a place . . . '

'And that's now.' I wanted to alleviate Sujay's fear. 'Come on. I'll do it and you can just follow on. I'll get away with it easier than you.'

I approached the first table where there was a party of Americans.

'You see that gentleman over there?' I pointed out Guruji. 'He just wants you to know how much he loves you.'

'How nice!' They seemed amused by the interruption. 'Who is he?'

'A spiritual teacher who has come to help us.' I spoke as though this was an everyday occurrence.

'Well, do give him our thanks and wish him well.'

'I will.'

The next table was filled with locals and I realized there was going to be a language problem. I began to point and gesture.

'That man . . . he loves you.' And I clasped my hands over my heart with all the passion that I could muster, thinking that at least I could entertain them with a bit of theatre. Laughter rippled around each of the tables in turn as I went about my mission, finding different ways of expressing Guruji's sentiments to the assorted crowd. Sujay kept close behind. When we got to the final table I realized that Guruji had become the focus of everyone's attention in the restaurant. Of course . . . that is what he had wanted – to be watched. Not for *his* sake but for *theirs*. I had seen him behave like this before, but now it dawned on me that he was enabling himself to be a channel to all those around him. They could feel his love, his sense of freedom, and they were enjoying the experience. His ability to express himself struck a chord deep within their hearts. We all wanted to be free within ourselves, whether we realized it consciously or not.

I noticed that some musicians had begun to play and one of them was demonstrating a Greek dance with great bravado. I realized that Guruji would not let any opportunity pass him by. I looked again and saw Guruji approaching the singer.

'Shall I sing for you, or dance?'

'Which ever you like.' The man was too bewildered to object.

None of us could believe how the waiters, musicians and guests accepted the situation so benignly. He had not only succeeded in disturbing everyone's meal, but was now interrupting their evening's entertainment. The musicians accompanied him as best they could, as he sung his way through a number of Indian prayers and love songs. Our own party reacted in different ways: some were angry because they wanted to listen to the Greek music, others recoiled with embarrassment, some got drunk, while others sat back amused. I was surprised to find that I was remarkably unaffected by the play. I trusted Guruji. I believed that he knew exactly what he was doing, but that it was just beyond our powers of comprehension. The more Guruji sang, the more filled with emotion his voice became. It seemed as though he would never stop . . .

Then, suddenly, from somewhere behind me, I heard a commotion in the crowd. I looked around and saw Sujay moving forward. I could see tension in his face. He marched across the dance floor towards Guruji. 'That's it. Enough is enough.' There was anger in his voice. 'Party time's over Guruji. We're off.'

He promptly took the microphone from him and returned it to the singer with an apology for any inconvenience that had been caused. Then, as though he were ticking off a naughty child, Sujay took Guruji's arm and led him firmly to the exit.

The celebration was over.

Later that night I looked for Sujay but he was nowhere to be found. After much searching, I eventually discovered that he had taken refuge in Tony's apartment.

'How could I have done that Usha?' Sujay implored me for an answer, some consolation, as soon as he saw me.

'Easily Sujay . . . easily.'

'I just couldn't take any more.'

'Are you surprised? We all felt exposed. At least you did something about it, and that took courage.' I wanted to comfort him as he had once comforted me.

'No Usha, it was not courage but fear that made me do it. I was afraid of what all those other people in the restaurant were thinking.'

And there lay the irony. Sujay, the ex-marine who had faced horrendous wartime dangers in Vietnam, had been made to confront his own fear in a Cyprus restaurant by the masterful play of his guru. As he lay there, smitten by the experience, Sujay appeared vulnerable and child-like.

'Sujay, at least you have the courage to face it. I admire you so much for that. Most people spend their whole lives running away from their fear. At least we're trying to overcome it.' And I took his hand and squeezed it. He appeared filled with remorse, not so much for his action but for the fear that had instigated it. I felt waves of love go out to him.

'All we have to cope with now is the airport practice.' Roopa knew the routine well, and had developed a sense of humour to help deal with the strange phenomenon of taking Guruji into public places. I decided to keep myself at a distance by chatting to the new friends that I had made during the last ten days. Across the airport lounge, the resonant voice rang out. 'Usha. Come here.'

I paced my steps slowly wondering what on earth Guruji

would get up to this time.

'Yes?'

'You see the man over there?' Guruji pointed to a young swarthy-looking man who was wearing headphones. 'I want you to give him my address in South Africa. Ask him to write to me.'

I knew that I would never see the man again, so I was not in the least bit bothered about delivering the message. In fact I was intrigued. The only problem I could envisage was getting his attention as he seemed to be well away with his music. I went over and tried to catch his eye.

'Excuse me.'

'Yes?'

'You see that Indian gentleman over there in the suit?'

'Yes . . . I was wondering who he was.'

'He has asked me to give you his address in Capetown. He says you may want to write to him.'

'He must have been reading my thoughts. Who is he?'

'Gururaj Ananda Yogi – a spiritual teacher.'

'Tell him how grateful I am. I've been looking for someone like that for some time now. I'll write to him. Thank you.'

My flesh tingled as we looked at each other, both amazed by the encounter. On the way home, I wondered whether any of us would ever be able to understand the Cyprus experience . . .

I returned to Dent in turmoil. Already the time away seemed distant, confused and unreal. There was no point in even trying to rationalize it: I only had two weeks before Guruji returned from his American tour to give the British course. I knew that this would be quite a different experience. To my relief Rachel decided to come too; I liked the thought of having family support. She had remained devoted to Guruji throughout the years I had been away from him and had been delighted when I had finally got back in touch. Apparently there was quite a large contingent of younger people who attended courses now. The two stalwarts from the old days were Peter, a retired Maths teacher, and his wife Jean. Apparently they had watched the movement go through momentous changes as Guruji had altered his teaching methods over the years. It comforted me to know that they were still around.

It was not long after we had arrived on the course, that Guruji intimated that he wanted me to look after him. Vidya and Roopa had remained in the States and, although Rajesh and Jasmini were competent in the role, it was clear that for some reason Guruji wanted me close by. I quickly learned my tasks. I not only had to take notes on any teaching that took place spontaneously, but I also had to arrange personal interviews and healings, look after his guests, as well as act as his shield and nurse. I soon realized how frail he was. On the first evening he lost his balance and would have fallen headlong if two of us had not been there to catch him. The incident made me acutely aware of my responsibility. Guruji tried to ease my mind.

'It's the spiritual force that keeps my body going. Only when my work is done will my body give up.'

In between *satsangs* Guruji would discuss teaching problems, perform healings, select individual practices for new meditators, and devise more advanced practices for those of us who had been around for a number of years. Whenever I disappeared to have a bath or change, someone came looking for me. I quickly learned that Guruji wanted me there at his side at all times and soon realized that this was a discipline for me: I had to remember to think of his needs before my own. But whenever I heard the words, 'Usha, where were you?', I felt such waves of love radiating from him, that I never felt my duty to be a chore. Just as he wanted me to understand his needs, he always seemed to know mine . . . usually before I knew them myself. 'Usha needs her notebook, some fruit, a glass of wine, to see how Rachel is . . . fetch Rachel here.' Rachel came to his room tentatively. She would sit on the floor beside him and he would take her head in her hands and look into her eyes. She was just twenty years old.

'You are like a daughter to me Rachel.' Her face softened and she seemed to melt into his. 'Do you understand what that means? I want to be proud of you . . . I want you to be happy . . . so, so happy.' He got up from the chair and turned to face her. 'Rakhi . . . Rakhi – it's your spiritual name. It means the protector of your brother . . . it's symbolized by a tie that you wear on the wrist. Rakhi – the one who cares for others. That's you my darling. You're very special to me, do you know that?'

Sometimes during the day he would turn on me unexpectedly.

'Empty the waste-paper basket Usha.'

'But it's not full.'

'Usha, get rid of the rubbish.'

I took the basket outside immediately, realizing that he wanted me to get rid of the rubbish within myself.

Other times he would turn to me softly and ask: 'Why do you love me, Usha?'

Bewildered by the question I would hesitate: 'Because . . . .'

'No 'because'. All reasons are of the mind and love is of the heart. You love because you love, because you love . . . it is a continual flow. Do you understand that, my darling?'

When he was supposed to be resting in the afternoon, sometimes he would prefer to gaze into my eyes, as though he were radiating energy to somewhere far out in the Universe.

'While we are here Usha, the ripples of energy go far beyond the confines of these walls. All the people who are sick and suffering need to be touched and healed by Love. There is so much work to be done . . . so much.'

I began to realize that it helped him to have another person to focus on. Between the two of us a circuit of energy was created that allowed the spiritual force to flow more powerfully. The more time I spent with him, the more I realized how easy it was for him to slip away into deep meditation - a state of *samadhi*. Increasingly it was becoming more difficult for him to remain on the same plane as us for any length of time.

When the course came to an end, he did not want me to leave. I kept insisting that my lift would depart without me. 'I'm expected downstairs Guruji . . . I have to go. Goodbye . . . '

'Usha, don't go so soon. You are my light, my life . . . the channel through which my love flows.'

I was touched by his words and realized how much I would

miss him during the following months. 'Until the autumn,' I said buoyantly, as a way of lifting his spirits as well as my own. I pulled myself away and left.

On the way home I laughed at the absurdity of the situation. Who was I to cheer up my teacher? It was I that needed help – not him. Yet I was bewildered as to why he persisted in making me feel so special. Surely this was not the role of a spiritual master? I wanted to let go of my ego-self, not have it bolstered.

But who could understand the ways of the masters? And how could one ever explain them?

The beauty of a cave is in its nothingness – the empty space that is left when the hard surfaces have been dissolved away over long periods of time. Similarly, it is the combination of subtle erosion along with occasional bouts of more brutal abrasion, that eventually succeeds in breaking down our own outer walls of resistance.

Only when they have finally been dismantled can the nature of our true Self shine through . . . that nothingness in which everything is contained.

8

It took a while for rumours surrounding the future of the Outdoor Centre to become more than hearsay. We had known that cut-backs were imminent, but it was uncertain as to whether these would involve the instructors losing their jobs. Eventually messages filtered through that the Centre was to close so, when John's redundancy notice arrived, our future was in question. Over the years I had worked in both village pubs and the tea-shop as a way of earning extra money to support ourselves and buy extra film and photographic materials. But I was reluctant to increase my hours, as I knew that I would have little time either for photographic work or meditation teaching.

'What are we going to do?' I expected John to have an answer.

'I'm not sure. I don't want to move away from Dent.'

'I don't either. But you'll have to get some work. We can't manage without regular income.' I could sense my old insecurities surfacing.

'I'm aware of that.'

'So what will you do then?' I persisted.

'I don't know.'

His evasion frustrated me and I tried to pin him down. 'What would you *like* to do?'

'I'd like to pursue the photography.'

'But we won't be able to make enough money from that.'

'Maybe. But you asked me what I'd like to do and that was my answer.'

Shortly afterwards I went to stay with my sister and her husband, Tony. Once again the familiarity and cheerfulness of their household made a welcome refuge at this latest crisis point in my life. In the event, with the help of my brother-in-law, I gained a different perspective on our situation. He was a University English lecturer, but he had an eclectic range of interests. He moved with enviable ease and expertise through the different worlds of ornithology, flowers, jazz and drama which gave him a broader than usual vision on life. Because of our long friendship, Tony had the confidence to question me closely. 'Why do you rely on John to make the decision about your future? Surely you have equal responsibility.'

'John has a good degree, work experience in different fields and so on. The only jobs that I have earned money from are pulling pints and washing up in the pubs of Dent. I don't have any qualifications.'

'Then why don't you get some?'

I was surprised by the question. I had never thought of becoming a student again. Indeed, why should John assume the responsibility of earning our income? I was not overly drawn to the idea as I knew that I would get jealous if he were off with his camera each day. Nevertheless, I felt ashamed that the possibility had not even crossed my mind. I looked to Tony for advice. 'What could I do?'

'How about a degree? You'd get a lot out of it and Lancaster University isn't far away from Dent.'

'And study what? They'd never have me.'

My lack of confidence showed but Tony was encouraging. 'Maybe you could read English? You like words and writing.'

'I'm not sure that I could take the endless analysing of texts.'

'Then what about Religious Studies? It would tie in with your meditation interests – and they have a good department there.'

His suggestion intrigued me. I had wanted to learn more about different religions for some time now: I was curious to see how each perceived and explained the philosophy that I had glimpsed through experience. I mused that I could go on to study the lives of the mystics.

Tony explained: 'You'd be able to specialize as you went through the course.'

'But would they have me? I've no appropriate pieces of paper.'

'I know that you'd make a good student.'

It was Tony's positive attitude that persuaded me that it was worth a try.

It did not take long for me to arrange an interview at Lancaster University. I was encouraged by the fact that John and I had just completed our second photographic essay – this time on the Lake District. The success of this latest venture gave me the confidence to explain to the admissions tutor that I wanted to equip myself better to write and produce books. Whether it was our mutual interest in photography and recording local life, that ensured we got on well I was not sure; but, on the basis of an animated conversation, he decided to offer me a place.

John was bemused. 'How will a Religious Studies degree enable you to make money?'

I had not given that much thought. 'Perhaps I could teach? It's too early to say.'

'True. But I wouldn't like you to think that after three years of study you'll be paying our way. I believe in scholarship as an end in itself – I don't think a degree has to lead anywhere in particular. If I were you I'd make the most of it and just enjoy it.'

'I'm sure I will. It's time I did more reading and studying, and I'm curious to find out more about different religions. Who knows, I may begin to understand Guruji better?'

'I doubt you'll ever do that.'

'Why not?'

'Nobody in their right minds would have put up with what you did in Cyprus. The whole time sounds crazy.'

'That's the role of a true master. To shake us up – to shake us out of our minds.'

'I'd prefer to hang on to mine.'

'But it's our minds that cause us our problems. They're so cluttered up with opinions that we can't see clear of them. The role of a master is to jolt us out of our thinking patterns so we have a less restrictive view of the world. But the means they use to do that are often obscure. That's why so little is known about the ways of the masters: the guidance they give is so often misunderstood. Guruji has come to help ordinary people like you and me. There's no need for us to take ourselves away from the world to progress spiritually. On the contrary, our interaction with the world can be used as a catalyst to make us search deeper.'

'I'm happy as I am – I like the way I see the world.'

John appeared so confident in his beliefs that I felt intrusive challenging them at all – but occasionally I was tempted to nudge him a little. 'Come on John – everyone can be happier . . . we can all get more out of life.'

'And how will seeing the world differently help with that?'

'By ridding ourselves of restrictions we can live fuller and freer lives – that's what I want anyway. We can also empathize more with other people. Being caught up in our mind makes us judge people and that's an act of separation. We need to realize that we're all the same underneath . . . all part of that One consciousness. I want to experience that.'

'Then explain how Guruji's playing around helps you to do that.'

'It's simple. His actions make me look at my re-actions.' I paused for a while. I wanted to elucidate my ideas but I knew how easy it is to get lost in words. 'You see we're different. You believe in just getting on with life and enjoying it as you can. That's OK for you. But I want to open myself up so I can experience deeper levels of love . . . that unifying love which underlies all existence. For me, this is what the spiritual path is all about. But to achieve that, I have to remove all the barriers from within myself. Instead of giving opinions and judging others, I have to see the effect the world has on me. Whenever I feel pinched, angry, sore or fearful, I know there's a block inside me that needs resolving. It's events *outside* that make me look at the tensions *inside*. Life's full of teachings – all that a spiritual master does is to accelerate the process of life so that we can learn more quickly.'

'How on earth can he do that?'

'By creating situations that make us look at ourselves. But only a true mystic – someone who has walked the complete path to the goal – is able to do that. The essential difference between a true master and a fraud, is that the former encourages you to find yourself, while the latter wants you to follow him. But the process wouldn't work if the student wasn't committed to understanding more about themselves. Guruji's behaviour would drive most people mad . . . as it does me sometimes. But I want to break out of my boundary walls. What Guruji offers us are not only the tools to open ourselves up, but also a reflection of what's inside. He serves as our mirror.'

'If Guruji were a mirror, he'd have to be all things to all people.'

'That's exactly what he is, John.'

'I can't accept that.'

'No . . . I'm not sure that I can.' I was always relieved when I stopped presenting my case. 'How can I explain what I don't truly understand myself? Come and ask Guruji yourself.'

'I might just do that.'

When Guruji came to England I had already begun my studies at Lancaster, but nothing would prevent me from attending the course. John decided to bring Abigail and Charlotte along for the first few days – however it was not until the day of John's departure that an occasion arose for him to talk to Guruji. The morning *satsang* had ended and a few of us went back to Guruji's room.

'John, I want to ask you something.' Guruji looked serious.

'Ask away.' I could tell that John's display of confidence belied his apprehension as to what Guruji was going to say.

'I would like you to take care of Usha for me.'

John's relief showed: 'I'll do my best.'

'You are her caretaker for this lifetime. Will you remember that?'

'How could I forget?'

'It's important . . . I want her to be happy.' Guruji paused. 'What work are you doing now?'

'I suppose technically I'm out of a job, but I'm managing to get some freelance instructing work.'

Again Guruji fell silent before he spoke. 'I'll tell you what you can do . . . '

'Please. I would appreciate that.' I could hear the hint of sarcasm in John's voice.

Proudly Guruji stood back to announce his idea. 'You can sculpt!'

John looked aghast. 'Excuse me . . . what?'

'Become a sculptor, John.'

'But I can't sculpt.'

'You like rock and caves, don't you?'

'Yes, but they're sculpted by nature. I wouldn't know where to begin.'

'Don't worry . . . I'll tell you what to do.' Guruji spoke slowly while the rest of us sat back, smiling at his latest idea. 'You take a piece of rock, stone or whatever. Then with a hammer and chisel you gently tap and chip until a form appears. It's at this point that you begin to create your rock into a work of art. You feel what is emerging and respond to whatever that is – it may be a person, an animal or an object of some kind . . . it's not important. Then you carve and rub down . . . carve and rub down . . . like this.' And he moved his arm in a circling motion to demonstrate. 'You do this until the object is perfected – its essence realized. That's how a sculpture is done. I tell you, it's simple. I'll buy the first one, John.'

By the time Guruji had finished his explanation we were all laughing. Yet I was aware that there was deeper meaning to his jest. Had he not just offered us a brilliant exposition of the process of unfoldment?

'I'm flattered,' John said looking puzzled. 'But why do you think I'd be any good at sculpting?'

'You would. I can see it in you.'

'How?'

'Your heart will respond to the rock. It will be a spiritual practice for you.'

John sensed an opening here. 'What do you mean by 'spiritual'?'

'The spiritual force is that which allows you, me and the entire Universe to exist.'

'I don't understand what you're saying. I don't feel that there's anything spiritual about me.'

'My beloved son . . . you radiate it. I can see it flowing through you.'

'But I don't *feel* it.'

'Just let go . . . allow yourself to feel it. Sculpting will help you. You are a beautiful soul, John. I can see it as you're standing there in front of me. Come my son . . . ' And Guruji went up to him, opened his arms, and gave him a warm embrace.

John appeared flushed, moved by the attention that he was receiving. He waited a moment before taking his leave but Guruji stopped him. 'You can't go yet John – you've had no lunch. It's a long journey and you need some food in your stomach. Usha tells me that it's your birthday so we can sing the birthday song. Come on . . . let's have a party.'

More places were set for lunch, and the celebrations began.

When the time finally came for John and the children to leave, Charlotte said her goodbyes first. She was seven and had enjoyed sitting close to Guruji during his talks – that is until he had asked her to sing a prayer with him. She was shy, so the request had appeared daunting. Gently Guruji had spent much of the *satsang* coaxing her to respond, until eventually Charlotte could just be heard singing '*Jai Ram*' down the microphone.

So, Guruji's parting words to her were not without meaning: 'You'll make a great actress, Charlotte.'

Then he took Abigail in his arms. She was twelve and had a sensitive, almost secretive demeanour. Her dark hair and eyes enhanced this aspect of her nature.

'Oh Abigail . . . if only my youngest son Beran could meet you. He would fall in love . . . '

I noticed her eyes fill with tears. Neither of them wanted to leave. Guruji had succeeded in reaching out and touching them deep inside, and they had been moved by the experience. As I went to see them off, Guruji shouted after us. 'Don't be long with your goodbyes. I want Usha back here quickly. And remember John, the first sculpture is mine.'

I had grown more at ease with my role of taking care of him. I now accepted that he wanted me with him at all times, even when he was listening to the personal concerns of others. In return for this trust, I did my best to ensure that those who needed to see him had the opportunity of doing so, and I watched and learned while he was with them. One day Breeyana, a woman from Belgium, came to talk to Guruji about her son who had difficulty hearing in one ear. After they had discussed the problem, Guruji sat back in his chair and looked her over.

'Get rid of all this.' Guruji spoke in a relaxed manner, yet even so I was taken aback by his effrontery. Breeyana dressed boldly. She wore a black leather jacket with large padded shoulders, had jewellery that was chunky and daring, and her nails were painted bright red.

'What do you mean Guruji?' She asked in astonishment.

'All this.' He waved his hand again, indicating clearly that he meant her style of clothes and make-up.

'But why?' She tilted back her hands to admire her nails. 'I like this colour.'

'There's no need for it.'

'Why not?'

'Just be yourself.'

'I am. And I like to wear it.'

I caught Breeyana's eye and we smiled at each other. It was refreshing to find someone who was not afraid to answer Guruji back. Many would have slunk away in search of the nail varnish remover. But not Breeyana. Boldness was her nature and she had no fear of expressing it, whether it was through her clothes or her responses to Guruji. After a little more banter she left the room good-humouredly.

After she had gone Guruji turned to the rest of us there. Out of the blue he said: 'Breeyana should lead the organization in Belgium.'

There was a cry of disbelief. 'But she's only just learned to meditate.'

'No matter. She will help many people in Belgium. Can she be instructed in the procedures while she is here?'

The decision was accepted and later that day Breeyana was asked if she would like to take on the role. She was clearly astonished. 'Does he expect me to remove my nail varnish?'

'No Breeyana. You are you – he wants you to be yourself,' I informed her confidently.

'That's OK then. I'll do it.' And she gave one of her broad, beautiful smiles.

One afternoon, when we were alone together, Guruji took the opportunity of asking me about my studies at Lancaster. 'Do you think that you're going to find God there, Usha?'

'No. But I might learn more about different religions and belief systems. Who knows . . . it might help me to understand *you* better? At present I'm writing an essay entitled – *I am Siva.*'

'And what are you saying?'

'I'm writing about the totality of life.'

> *The Hindu god Siva represents the wholeness of life. Every aspect of life is contained within him and expressed through him. It is because of Siva's all-embracing nature that humankind is able to relate and respond to him so easily. Opposition and paradox permeate all the stories about Siva: he represents destruction and procreation, is the ascetic and the lover, the protector and the feared one, the philosopher and also the wild card who dances on the mountain tops. Siva's nature is to assume all forms, take on all roles and act out the full range of emotions – in this way he becomes all things to all people. Siva symbolizes the totality of life. Through discovering the truth about Siva, we can discover the truth about ourselves.*

For me, Guruji played that role. He contained all aspects of life but was not attached to any of them. He entered into the full play of life, yet also remained the observer. In so being, he became a mirror for us to see ourselves. He was the clear reflector. Although I knew that Life was full of teachings from which we could learn, through Guruji I was able perceive a sharper image of myself. Without my darker areas being reflected back at me, how would I know what they were or where they concealed themselves? What I saw was not always comfortable or pleasant, but I had not pursued the spiritual path in order to be puffed up. Quite the contrary – I wanted my trappings to be stripped away.

But the process of uncovering one's True Self is a risky business. Two-headed monsters can appear unexpectedly and take the student by surprise.

The last afternoon, while Guruji was asleep, I took the chance of slipping back to my bedroom to pack my belongings in readiness for our departure. I wanted to avoid the usual hiatus that occurred whenever I left him for too long, so this seemed an opportune moment – he would never realize. It had been arranged that I would go to Rajesh and Jasmini's for the weekend before Guruji flew off to the States. As fast as I could, I shoved my clothes into a bag and returned to Guruji's room. As I opened the door, I saw Guruji sitting by the window having a cup of tea. How stupid of me – of course he would know that I had gone.

I was shocked: my own deception stared back at me. In my mind I reasoned that I had had to pack, but in my heart I knew that I had avoided asking him because I did not want to cope with his gentle barracking. The situation was absurd. Of course he would not have minded my going to collect my things. But nevertheless, in that one misplaced act, I had been brought face to face with my dislike of uncomfortable situations.

Why did fears from the past have such a persistent hold over us that they influenced us so strongly now? No wonder people behaved unpredictably at times.

I stumbled with my excuses: 'I'm sorry . . . I just slipped away to pack. I thought you were sleeping. I should have told you where I was going. It was silly of me . . . I just couldn't face a scene. I'm sorry, really I am.'

Guruji sat there impassively listening to my outburst. I expected a reprimand but he gave me none. I imagined some comfort but he remained silent. For me, he was that mirror.

I sat in the back of the car directly behind Guruji. As Rajesh drove us away from the course, Guruji reached out for my hand and squeezed it reassuringly. 'Are you alright, Usha?'

'Yes Guruji.' He then closed his eyes and remained in meditation until we reached London.

The weekend flew by. It was filled with fun – the singing of Indian prayers, the painting of pictures, the impersonation of different characters from Hitler to Gandhi, and the relishing of a variety of delicious Indian dishes prepared by Jasmini. It was an experience of joyous interaction when, for a short while, all of us let go of worldly cares and responsibilities in order to laugh and play. And together we celebrated my fortieth birthday.

An hour or so before I was due to catch my train, Guruji became quiet and self-absorbed. I respected these times, acknowledging that something deeper was going on that was beyond my comprehension. I sat on the floor beside him and rested my head on his knee. Together we were silent and my mind became still. After a little while, Guruji raised his head and stared straight ahead of him. It seemed as though he was piercing the veils of the future. 'Usha,' he whispered.

'Yes Guruji.'

Guruji's voice became so soft that I had to strain to hear him, but it seemed important that I heard what he was saying.

'Ananda was one of Buddha's closest disciples . . . do you know why the Buddha pushed Ananda away before he died, Usha?'

His words were left hanging in the air. The stillness of the scene was too great for my mind to think coherently. I murmured something about attachment, which was the only thought that fleetingly came into my mind. At the time I could neither fathom the depth of his question, nor understand what my response should be. I was brought back from the silence by feeling Guruji's arm gently encouraging me to move away. He motioned me to sit in the chair opposite him.

'Jasmini, will you give Usha a healing?'

I was surprised by his request. I had been with Guruji for almost a week now, so why should I need Jasmini to heal me? I was well and strong within myself, filled with the love that Guruji had bestowed on me. As I sat opposite Guruji, I looked at him questioningly. Why? What is happening? I then closed my eyes and felt Jasmini place her hands on my head.

When I put my bags in the car ready for departure, I noticed that Guruji had pulled back the sitting-room curtains. He smiled, blew kisses, and waved his hand vigorously to say goodbye.

I called out to him. 'Goodbye Guruji, goodbye. Thank you for everything . . . until the spring.' And Rajesh and I drove off to the station.

When I arrived home late that night, Guruji telephoned to see that I arrived safely. 'Did you cry Usha?'

'How did you know?'

'I heard you crying.'

I had just had an uncontrollable outpouring of tears that seemed to well up, not from sadness, but from some phenomenal need for release. I was confused by the outburst. John had put his arms around me and held me tight. 'Don't worry – I'll look after you,' he murmured quietly.

I enjoyed my new routine at Lancaster. Studying in the library, the challenge of essay-writing, discussions with young and lively minds, all focused my mind in a way that it had not been for years. I quickly realized that any understanding of eastern religions that I had hoped to gain, was bound to be limited. How could the world of academia possibly explore the realms of spiritual experience? Its role was to research different forms. I consoled myself that I was fortunate in having experience as well.

But it was while I was at Lancaster that I met Jill – a kind, unassuming woman, who at first gave the impression that she lacked confidence in herself. She had a quality of innocence about her that I found endearing and I was drawn to get to know her better. It was not long before she expressed an interest in learning meditation; but, concerned that a teaching programme might distract me from studies, I was reluctant to teach her at first. It was her insistence that eventually made me acquiesce. Yet, how would I have known that through this seemingly inconsequential meeting that so much would be gained? Around Jill, a circle of meditators was to grow through whom I would learn far more, through interaction and sharing, than I did in all my time of academic study. Jill was to become the prize jewel of my time in Lancaster – a focal point for my future teaching and learning.

The only break that I had planned from my work was to go and see Guruji again in March: there was so much I wanted to ask him now. Vidya was coming over from the States so I looked forward to seeing her too. However, I did not get the chance of seeing either of them before the first evening's talk. I was sitting in the middle of the hall and it was not long before Guruji noticed me. 'Usha, there you are.' He beckoned me. The tone of his voice was strangely flat, considering that I had not seen him for several months. I went up to him, but he seemed aloof and I felt uncomfortable. I returned to my seat as soon as possible. I found it difficult to believe that he had scarcely acknowledged me. I was prepared for the fact that Vidya would assume the role of carer now that she was here, but not for Guruji's change in attitude towards me.

As the second day moved into the third I felt increasingly threatened by the way that Guruji was treating me. It seemed as though he had ceased to know me. The story that he had told me of Ananda occasionally flitted across my mind. Was it being enacted now? Each time he ignored me, it was as though I was being struck down. He looked through me instead of at me, pretending that I was not there. Was this real or was it a game? Was he ill – had his memory relapsed? Or was his behaviour deliberate? I could not tell. He just seemed to have forgotten who I was.

While trying to cope with my overwhelming feelings of rejection, I also had to look after some meditators from Dent who had come on their first course. They wanted to meet Guruji in person so that they could gain more understanding of his teachings. But in every *satsang* Guruji disappointed them. He might respond to a question briefly, but then he would quickly move on to an hour's worth of light entertainment. 'Charles. Why don't you give us a song?'

Charles was a similar age to Guruji and had known him for many years. He also had an excellent voice and knew a lot of music-hall songs. Amiably Charles went to the microphone and, with one arm clutched to his breast, began his repertoire: '*I'll take you home again, Kathleen . . .*'

'That was great Charles,' Guruji said clapping. 'Give us another.'

And Charles would launch off into a ballad or folk song, in an attempt to please Guruji. When he had finished we assumed that the *satsang* would resume as normal, but no – Guruji would then ask someone else to come out and perform, and so it went on until the time was up. I was at a loss to explain this latest aspect of his teaching to my friends. All I could think of was that my reputation in Dent would be ruined. This was hardly what they had expected from their spiritual teacher. They wanted words of wisdom yet, in their eyes, they were getting what they could hear better in their own village hall.

One afternoon it was arranged that we would meet in small groups to discuss the course. The occasion provided a window of opportunity in which Guruji's many different ways of teaching could be explained to the newcomers. As I assembled with my group of meditators I was dismayed to find that we had been assigned the room directly outside Guruji's dining-room. I knew that if he realized we were there, there was every chance that we would be invited in. No sooner had we sat down than Guruji came out to greet us. 'Come and join us. You're not sitting out here while we're eating.'

'But we're having a meeting, Guruji,' I protested vainly.

Yet again he ignored me, and proceeded to usher our group inside. I took the seat directly behind Guruji so that I would not have to face him. The rest of our party sat around the room infuriated that they had been denied the chance of talking amongst themselves.

'Listen,' Guruji said over his bowl of soup. 'I'm going to tell you the secret of life . . . '

Guruji spoke alluringly, as though at last he was going to reveal some precious nugget of information that was going to satisfy his audience. Please, I thought to myself, just say one thing that will be helpful to these people . . . just a few words of wisdom that will give them comfort and inspiration when they go home. That is what they have come for – this is what they expect. There was a long pause while we waited in anticipation. Guruji began to drum the table with his fingers as an overture to his speech. He spoke slowly: 'The secret of life is . . . is. . to have fun! Do you not see the deep meaning in this teaching?'

No Guruji, I do not. I felt anger burn up inside me. How can you so effectively destroy the hopes of these people, and simultaneously wreck whatever reputation I have left in my home village? How can you treat me like this? It is as though you never knew me. All the times we have spent together, all the times that I have sat next to you at this very table – serving your guests, taking notes for you, making sure that you have everything you need. And now it is as though I never existed. I wanted to escape to my room, but I knew that it would create even more of a scene if I did. Instead I tried to take my mind away from the situation by sharing some jokes with the person sitting next to me.

Guruji immediately swung round. 'Be quiet, Usha. Pay attention when I speak.'

I froze and then relaxed. At least I had got his attention.

But I felt wretched inside. I was miserable and afraid. To whom could I turn for help? Guruji was no longer there for me. In my more sanguine moments I reasoned that he was pushing me away deliberately, that this was a test, that he genuinely wanted me to be free of any attachment to him. I told myself that my task was to brace myself against the force of his rejection, but I found it so hard to do. His love had been so overwhelming that to have it withdrawn so completely was more than I could bear. I decided to turn to Jean for help. She was like a mother to us all and had known Guruji for as long as I had. I asked her if she would give me a healing to help me regain my strength.

'Do you want to talk first?'

'Perhaps . . . ' I hesitated, unsure of what to say.

'I understand what you're going through. Rejection is so painful,' Jean said sympathetically.

'It's as though he never knew me.'

'I know.'

'I thought I could cope but I can't,' I tried to explain my dilemma.

'Don't try and cope, Usha.'

'What do you mean?'

'Give yourself permission to be vulnerable. It's alright *not* to be alright.'

Her words struck me, but nevertheless I found myself protesting. 'But I should be strong enough to take it, shouldn't I?'

'There are no medals for burying one's feelings and pretending they're not there. We have to be open and pay them some attention.'

'I feel that Guruji is testing me and I'm failing abysmally . . .'

'And it's alright to fail. How would anyone remain unaffected by what he's putting you through?'

'But I'm afraid. It's as though he's negating my whole being.'

'I know Usha, and it's important for you to accept those feelings and not to deny them. It's through our own suffering that we learn to have compassion for others. It's alright to be weak – it's through acknowledging our weakness that we discover true strength. Come on now, I'll give you a healing.'

I left her room feeling as though I was treading on glass. I hardly dared take a step for fear that my fragile world might break apart. I went back to my room to bathe and found a note from Vidya lying on my bed. It was brief:

> *Dearest Usha,*
> *How can you be so strong with all that you're going through?*
> *I feel so weak beside you. I'd love the chance to talk to you*
> *sometime. Please find time. Love Vids*

I smiled to myself. I wanted to go and find her and tell her how desperately I had been hurt. I wanted to explain that my strength was a façade, a show put on to impress Guruji . . . to try and win back his love. With renewed courage I went to Guruji's room and came across Vidya in the corridor outside. I called to attract her attention.

'Usha, how good to see you. I want to talk to you but we never seem to get the chance.'

'I feel I have to keep away,' I began to explain.

'I can't believe what you're going through.'

'I just don't want you to think that I'm finding it easy. I'm not. At times I feel desperate.'

'I get hurt when he sends me away just for a few hours,' Vidya consoled.

Our conversation was brought to a close by the appearance of Guruji in the doorway. 'What are you talking about? Please come in here.'

It felt strange to be in his room again under such altered circumstances. There were a few people about, so discreetly I settled myself on the sofa. Directly in front of me was a large bowl of fruit with some succulent-looking black grapes draped over the top of it. They looked tempting and, since I did not want to draw unnecessary attention to myself, I decided to take one without asking. No sooner had I picked one off than I heard Guruji's voice resounding across the room.

'Have a grape, Usha.'

Did he miss nothing? Could I not even sneak a grape without him knowing about it? Years later I was to reminisce about Guruji's 'grape awareness'.

'It's time that you got ready for *satsang*, Vidya,' Guruji reminded her.

As soon as she had gone, Guruji came and sat beside me. Although he was now close to me, it still felt as though he were a stranger. Yet, as soon as he spoke, I knew that his message was directed at me.

'Yesterday I sent Vidya away for a little while.' He paused as if to allow time for his words to sink in. 'I sent her away because she has to learn a lesson. The lesson is . . . that she is *nothing*.'

I shuddered as he uttered that final word. Once more the power of his energy cascaded through me. The atmosphere in the room became heavy and intense as each one of us tried to absorb the impact of his words. The silence was interrupted by Rajesh reminding us that it was time for us to go.

'Where is Vidya?' Guruji asked.

'She's having a wash and a change.'

'You are keeping us waiting, Vidya,' Guruji called out to her.

I was confused – both by what he had said and also by her delay. I would never have dared keep Guruji waiting. Why was he not reprimanding her? He simply put on his spectacles, leaned on his stick and waited patiently. I stood opposite him and looked across at him questioningly. I was bewildered. I did not understand Vidya's behaviour. My confusion was lodged so firmly in my mind that I knew Guruji must have picked up on it. But this time when I looked at him for an answer, there seemed to be no one there. It was as though I was looking directly through him. There was no person, no personality, just the empty shell of his body. His form had become a mask, an apparition. I no longer understood what was happening to him, to me or to anyone else. Please Guruji, explain . . .

I found comfort from my times with Rachel who again had taken leave from her nurse training to attend the course. I was glad to have her support. In the evenings we were always first in the bar.

'I can't take much more of this,' I confided in her.

'Yes you can. It's not your nature to give up.'

'It might be this time. What on earth are they going to say in Dent about a singing, dancing guru. Why is he doing it?'

'There must be a reason. I'm enjoying it anyway. It was fun doing the conga in and out of the meeting-hall last night.'

'For you, maybe. But imagine what it's like for someone who has never seen Guruji before. How could they ever take him or their meditation practices seriously again?'

'He's telling us to let go isn't he?' Rachel spoke as though she already knew the answer.

'I believe so . . . but the teaching is happening on so many different levels. He wants us to let go of everything – attachments, inhibitions, fears and needs – so that we can be truly free to be ourselves.'

'And it's working. I couldn't believe it when that old lady got up and sang the Eriskay love song. Imagine – that's been her life's ambition and at the age of seventy-five she realized it!'

'Yes, it was very moving. We have to hand it to him, he knows how to give us the medicine we need. It just doesn't always taste very nice. But I hate watching the disillusionment on the faces of the new meditators.'

'They're not your responsibility, Mum. They chose to come.'

I had always respected Rachel's insight. And since I did not want her to miss out on spending time with Guruji because of me, I was prompted to make a suggestion: 'Do you want to go to Guruji's room for the midnight meditation tonight?'

Rachel nodded. 'Only if you come too.'

'Alright then. I will.'

Guruji had devised a practice to show that in meditation we were all together, even though physically we may have been apart from one another. Around midnight everyone went to their own rooms to meditate on their own. The idea was that we would be able to experience the universal nature of that One consciousness. It was customary for a few people to go and meditate with Guruji, so it did not seem presumptuous for Rachel and me to go to his room at the appointed time. Others were already there. How different it seemed from the last course when Guruji had insisted that I sat right next to him. Just a few minutes into meditation he had pulled me towards him and had held me in his arms during the entire time. It had felt as though the force of Divinity was being channelled through him, through me, and on out to the rest of the world. Now, just a few months later, I was concerned about entering his room.

One or two people settled themselves cross-legged on the floor, while others sat on chairs. I noticed that Guruji placed himself near Rachel.

'Is it time? Shall we begin to mediate?' He said quietly.

We closed our eyes but, after a little, I was disturbed by a cry. It sounded like Rachel, so I opened my eyes to see if she was alright. I saw that Guruji had taken Rachel's hands and was entwining them in his. She appeared to be in a deep state of meditation while Guruji continued to move his arms around hers. I noticed that one or two others had opened their eyes to watch. Whether it was seconds or minutes that passed, I was not sure, but suddenly Rachel let out another cry that sounded sad and mournful. Then she cried out again, but this time the separate notes dissolved into one prolonged whimpering sound. I sat calmly, realizing that Guruji knew exactly what was going on. I understood that he was taking her through some experience to which none of us were a part. Eventually her crying quietened and he took her in his arms and she seemed at peace. It was not until later that she told me what had happened:

'The experience will always be with me. I think that he was letting me have a glimpse of his true nature. He took me out into the Universe where there was nothing but golden light. It was all so beautiful . . . so utterly peaceful. He took me away from myself and everything around me. But I wanted to stay there . . . I did not want to come back.' Rachel faltered, biting back her tears while she remembered. 'I looked down at Guruji and saw that he was *nothing*. He was just a form . . an empty shell. I did not want to come back to him or anything else. I believe he was showing me that he is just an open channel for all the light and love that is out there. But I wanted to stay there. It was the coming back that was so painful – that was why I cried . . . '

After all the emotional upheaval that had gone on, Rachel and I decided to make the most of the party on the last night of the course. We felt like dancing vigorously as a way of releasing all the tensions that had surfaced during the last few days. I had suffered and survived, and even grown used to Guruji's indifference towards me. It no longer seemed to bother me now. At one point during the evening Guruji composed a few lines.

Someone wrote them down and passed them to me.

It was a long time ago since I said 'I love you' – yet I know that even without a word, you feel in your heart that I do. The unspoken word of Love will forever be there . . . just know that we are together and that we belong to one another. That belonging will create the fire in our hearts which will consume us in the beauty of Love . . .

'Usha.' I was startled by him calling me. 'Could you and Vidya come to my room for a moment?'

We took an arm each and accompanied him upstairs. When we went in, he indicated that I should sit down on the bed. As he had done so often before, he knelt on the floor in front of me.

'Vidya, will you get Usha a drink?'

'Some water, please.'

I looked down at Guruji, desperately searching for some connection with him – a familiar look, a glance of recognition, something . . . anything of the relationship that we had once had. But still there was none.

'How are you feeling Usha? Do you have a problem?'

His tone was false and I was loath to respond. How on earth was I expected to express the pain that I had gone through during the last few days? Yet I wanted to say something, for he must have known how I had suffered.

I spoke matter-of-factly: 'I feel as though I have been punched in the stomach very hard.'

'I know Usha . . . I know.'

He took off my shoes and began rubbing my feet. 'Vidya and you are like sisters you know. Remember that, won't you.'

'I feel very close to her.'

'Usha, I have to move some energy.'

I reacted instinctively. 'No, please no.'

I could not take any more. I had had enough. I had succeeded in pulling myself up from the depths and was just beginning to feel myself again. I could not cope with any more emotional turmoil. I felt Guruji put his hand on my knee and move it up towards my right thigh. I tried pushing him away again crying out, 'Please don't. Leave me alone.'

But it was all over in an instant. He got up and I realized that I was free to go.

'Is that it Guruji?'

'Yes.'

'Goodnight then.'

'Goodnight, Usha.'

I wanted to escape to my room.

When I awoke the next morning the same overwhelming feelings of vulnerability had returned with a vengeance. I reassured myself that there was only one more *satsang* to sit through and then I could go home. But at that point I did not know the final twist to the story.

News broke that Guruji had decided he was not going to give his last talk: 'You must learn to take *satsang* yourselves,' he instructed calmly. A few people tried to persuade him otherwise, but he clearly had no intention of being there. I knew that there was no point in making more excuses to my meditators. All I could do was to offer my sympathy and say how wretched I felt myself. So that was it. The momentous five days had come to an end, and Guruji was due to leave at lunch-time. To everyone's surprise he was prompt in his departure. He came downstairs, moved slowly through the hallways, attentively saying his goodbyes to those who had gathered there. I knew that this was my last chance to re-establish contact with him. All I wanted was one last look of recognition, a loving goodbye, a memory of all those good times that we had spent together . . . I had to say something . . . even if it was just to thank him. I grabbed a pencil and paper and wrote a note, sensing that he would ignore me once more.

> *Dearest Guruji,*
> *Thank you for everything that you have ever done for me –*
> *I'm so grateful. I just never realized what a painful process it is*
> *. . . discovering what one is not. I love you, Usha.*

I thrust the note into Vidya's hand as she passed by. And there was Guruji standing close by. Once more he acknowledged everyone else but me. Again he looked through me as though I was not there. But this time, in the emptiness of that look, he seemed to strip away everything that I was, everything that I had ever stood for. All my thoughts, ideas, acts and defences – the very fabric that made up me – were suddenly wrought asunder, and I saw in reality that there was nothing there inside.

All my walls were down and I felt naked: no longer did I have anything to hide behind. In that one look he had succeeded in burning through all the layers of my ego-self. My web of illusion lay shattered in pieces around me. I saw that essentially I was *nothing*. It was *beyond* the ego that everything lay – God, Grace and the Ultimate experience of Love.

I could not wave him off. I stood alone in the corridor too stunned by the revelation, aware that I was not yet ready for that experience. Seemingly from nowhere, a young Irish girl ran up to me and said: 'I love Usha. You're such a beautiful person.'

'No,' I protested. 'It's not true.'

I realized the gulf that remained between God and me.

Ten days later Guruji telephoned me on his way back to South Africa from the States. It was the middle of the night. 'I just wanted to say goodbye, Usha. Do you remember the meaning of goodbye?'

'Of course. You have told us so many times.'

But he insisted on telling me again. 'It means *God be with you* . . . goodbye Usha.'

'Goodbye Guruji. Have a good journey.'

Outer forces may have to bombard the patterns from our past again and again, before eventually we become aware of them and they can be spiralled away. We tend to cling to the dross that surrounds us, for it makes us feel secure. But the process of dispersal gathers a momentum of its own and we have no power to stop it.

It is only when our tangled web has been totally dismantled, that we realize where our True Self lies.

9

As I walked across the University campus I breathed in deep. It was one of those May days when the air is so vibrant that I wanted to fill myself up with it. I was alive to the sensations around me. The clarity of the morning light enhanced the yellow-greens of the new foliage: the leaves shimmered and rustled as they were caught by the breeze. I flung my head back, opening myself up to the vastness of the sky. It was a day that invigorated and inspired. Because of it I worked well, absorbing the texts and writing up my commentary with an ease that was unusual. On my way home I stopped in Barbondale to watch the evening light play on the beck: water, grasses, rocks were all tinged with pink, while deep shadows were just beginning to cut across the sweep of fell above. When I arrived at the house, John was waiting for me in the doorway. His look of concern made me feel anxious.

'What's wrong?'

'I've got bad news for you, Eliza. Come and sit down.'

'What is it?' My mind raced through the possible alternatives – children, parents, a friend, what . . . who?

'I'm sorry but . . . Guruji died this morning.'

At first I could not assimilate what John had said. It seemed too surprising, too momentous a piece of information. I responded instinctively. 'Come, we must light candles and keep them burning through the night as a reminder that his light lives on. That's what Guruji did when Pavitrananda died.'

As I watched the candles burn, a calm washed through me. I

felt as though a tremendous energy had been released into the Universe, and a part of it had landed inside me. It seemed that through Guruji's death, a different quality of energy had been set in motion – life had been given fresh impetus, but in a way that was too subtle to fully comprehend. There was no sadness or tears – just a quiet, firm knowledge that Guruji was within me more strongly than ever before.

Had he not prepared me for this? I simply had not seen it at the time. The theme of the play was becoming clearer now: in the act of pushing me away, Guruji had tried to make me realize the importance of letting go of all attachments. There lay the essence of his teaching: he wanted us to stand on my own and know that we had all the resources within ourselves to overcome our fears and needs. All at once I felt overwhelmed with gratitude for everything that he had done for me. How many times had he told us that the role of a spiritual teacher is to wake us up to ourselves – to help us find the teacher within? I had been privileged to be taught these lessons by a masterful guru – now was my chance to discover how much I had learned.

I regarded it as my first duty to tell my new group of meditators in Lancaster about Guruji's death. One of them was Christa, a bright woman with clear blue eyes in her late twenties, who was not afraid of asking questions and giving opinions. As soon as I met her, I admired her openness. I broke the news to her gently, wondering what her reaction would be.

'That's a relief,' said Christa with a smile. 'He was the one bit of this teaching I found hard to take. You tell us that we can believe what we like, but then there's a guru behind it all – a male one at that! The idea made me feel distinctly uncomfortable.'

Of course. While Guruji was with us his personality was always in danger of obscuring his teachings – now they were free to stand on their own.

'I think we should all go and have a meal to celebrate,' I suggested, smiling to myself.

'Good idea.' And after a pause Christa added, 'By the way, I'm sorry.'

'You needn't be. I think it's for the best that he's gone.'

I was glad that she had told me of her doubts. Just as we had expressed our fears and feelings to Guruji, it was now our responsibility to encourage others to do the same to us. I knew that the relationship between the teacher and the taught was one of interaction and sharing and, through the process, we all learned more about ourselves. We were students of life together.

As soon as I had the chance, I escaped to the fells with my camera. I wanted to get back in touch with the earth again. 'Can I come and take some pictures with you Alan?'

'Come now. I'm going to check some yows and lambs for staggers. It's lack of calcium that does it. They just keel over and can be dead within hours.'

Together we rode to an intake high above Dentdale, bumping over the rough terrain on his four-wheeler. While he did the rounds of his sheep, I wondered at how little was known about the shepherd's life. Unless there was the commitment of going out with these people day after day, in all weathers, at all times of year, how was it possible to understand the life of the fell? As I sat there watching Alan, it occurred to me that it would make an exciting challenge for John and me to try and record their story. Not only did I want to get back to my photography again, but once more I wanted to relate to people who had a simple, straightforward approach to the world. I was beginning to see how easy it is to get so wrapped up in spiritual concepts, that ordinary life becomes in danger of losing its significance. I needed a firm reminder that spirituality and life are one.

Our publisher needed little persuading of the value of the project, while my tutor at Lancaster confirmed that one of the reasons for study was to open up opportunities for self-expression. So, after spending just a year exploring religion within the confines of the campus, I exchanged my Hindu and Buddhist texts for local expertise on what makes good tips, yows and mule gimmer lambs. Just a month after Guruji died, I left Lancaster.

'Can you be here at four in the morning? We're gathering for clipping and when it's warm t' sheep won't move in t' middle of the day.'

Each time we went out to gather, clip, dip, lamb or sell sheep, I felt privileged to be taken into this exclusive world. Hill farmers live differently: they have to make the fells work for them. Whether blizzards blow or the rain teems, they have to be out there checking their sheep, and John and I were determined to accompany them as much as we could. When we returned to the farmhouse, weary from a day's gather or a clipping, there was always the insistence that we should stay for tea. We loved the times spent sitting around drinking coffee, listening to the banter and adding to the local gossip. Tales were told and jokes made late into the night.

Whether it was time spent out on the fell or in the farmhouse, I became increasingly absorbed into their way of life. I laughed, I learned and photographed with new passion, as I felt moved by the love that these people had for the hills and their sheep. I got so engrossed with capturing farmyard scenes that I would step back . . . and back, and end up in the sheep-dip or the midden. Then the laugh would be on the other side. 'It's us who should have the camera now.' But afterwards there was deep concern about my state. 'Sheep dip's a nasty thing tha knows. You must tek good care of yeself.'

Whether it was an awkward lambing or a spate of ticks, I wanted to become totally involved in their concerns. When the snow drifted and buried sheep, I would take stick in one hand and camera in the other to ensure that I would not fall into the role of just being the observer. I wanted to be one of them. For me, these people had a direct approach to life that rang true. They lived on the cutting edge of changing weather, birth, and death – and I admired their strength and sense of fatalism.

From the fell I would return home to the warmth and familiarity of my own kitchen which, over the years, had become a gathering place for people to eat, drink and talk about life. Whether it was a new caving technique, some emotional trauma, a Lakeland recipe, or differing views on reincarnation, all topics were discussed with an enthusiasm that inspired. Home had become a place where both friends and family could lighten their load, against the background smells of baking bread and fresh coffee. The children accepted those who came and went with equanimity.

'If they're bearded they're cavers – if they hug us they're meditators.'

For the most part the children pursued their own lives, but were always there to support one another. There was an ease and playfulness between them, a natural rapport. The worst of their squabbles revolved around make-up and clothes, and I only needed to impose discipline when I feared for their safety. Increasingly, home and family became the mainstay of my life. Rachel returned to Dent on shorter breaks but, when possible, she preferred to travel abroad.

We were expecting her back from Portugal when she called. 'Can you pick us up at the station?'

'Us?' I enquired with curiosity.

'Eduardo's with me.'

Rachel had first met her Argentinian friend on a kibbutz in Israel three years previously. Since then he had travelled the world. As he was spending some time back in Europe, they had taken the opportunity to holiday together.

'I look forward to meeting him. How long is he staying?'

'I'm not sure.'

Would it be two weeks, a month or a year, I wondered to myself? Travellers had no commitments and I realized that he could be around for a while.

Eduardo greeted me in a thick Latin-American accent. 'Hello, how are you?'

The evocative smell of Gauloise lingered about him. In his black beret and with his shoulder-length dark hair, he reminded me of the Che Guevara posters. He seemed relaxed, easy-going and, with his striking Latin looks, I could see why Rachel had been attracted to him. When we got back to Dent a bottle of port was produced, and we chatted late into the night as was customary when one of the family returned from an adventure. The conversation oriented around different places that Eduardo had lived and worked.

'I have always managed to find a job . . . wherever,' he shrugged his shoulders. 'You think I will find one in Dent?'

Yes . . . he was obviously going to be around for a while. It seemed that my family had grown bigger overnight. I treated Eduardo as a son, supporting him in any way that I could. He was good-natured and fun. It was not long before he had found work in the pub, a caravan to live in, and had been welcomed into the local football team as the star who would help it win. 'It's that Argentinian foot-work that'll do it.' When Rachel came home on her days off from the hospital, there were now six of us around the table. And Eduardo loved the local dishes: over Cumbrian lamb with rowan jelly, washed down with a good red wine, we would sit and talk late into the night. With the Aga burning and the candles lit, the kitchen exuded a warmth that enhanced our feelings of togetherness. Such evenings were my happiest of times.

Whether it was Eduardo's expiring visa or Rachel's pregnancy that prompted them to marry, I was not sure. They said it was because they loved each other and I knew that to be true.

'Mum,' Rachel spoke decisively, 'we're going to Argentina. Eduardo hasn't been home for five years and I want to meet his family. We'll leave when the baby's born.'

The news cut through me like a knife. My first reaction was to use reason to try and dissuade them from going. 'But Rachel, you won't know anyone. Just imagine yourself in a strange country, stranded with a baby and unable to speak the language. It's difficult enough being constrained by a child when you're in a place that you know . . . but in Argentina you'll feel so alone. Eduardo, you've no idea what it'll be like for her.'

'My family will take good care of her – we're very close. And my sisters and brother have children of their own. You mustn't worry. She'll pick up the language quickly when she's living out there.'

'But it's so far away. We'll never see you.'

'Travelling is no big problem. I've done it for years.'

My attempt to reason gave way to emotional pleas. 'Please don't go for too long. I'll miss you. We haven't the money to travel that far – and what about the little one? I'll never see my grandchild. Rachel, we've always been so close . . . '

But it was too late. The decision had been made and it was not up to me to change it. It was a strange feeling, as though a part of me was going to be amputated unnecessarily. I had to learn to cope with the consequences – life in the north without them.

When Lucas was born, I showered him with all the love that I could in the time there was available. He was just five months old when they left. As we drove to the airport Eduardo sat in the back of the car with Lucas on his knee. He pursed his bottom lip downward in a funny habit that he had.

'Don't do that, Lucas,' Eduardo joked, 'you look like a mouse.'

I laughed and then I cried, as once again it hit home how much I was going to miss out on. All the good times that we had shared together were over. How had it happened that three such precious people were being taken so far away for me? The goodbyes are too painful to recount . . . the last embrace, the last wave, the last glance so full of longing, before disappearing behind the screen of the departure lounge . . . and those so dear to me were gone.

The pangs, the hurt, the pain of attachment tore away at me inside as if to say: See – you thought you were free? In my mind I knew that it was sensible for them to have a fresh start, for Eduardo to establish a career for himself. I could also see that it was good for Rachel to get right away from Dent and discover her husband's culture and language. But losing all three of them stunned me. All that closeness, companionship, laughter and fun, exploded apart so conclusively. What would life be like without them? How long would it take me to get used to it? Guruji's words resounded in my ears: 'Have attachments – nothing wrong with them. But don't be so attached that it causes you pain.'

On my way back up north, I broke my journey to stay with my sister. Their downstairs cloakroom was filled with an array of family pictures that had been taken over the last twenty years. Among them was one of Rachel that I had not seen before. The tears flowed again.

'Eliza,' Teresa consoled, 'there's a simple solution – just use the lavatory upstairs.'

As the evening wiled away, we got more drunk.

'It's not as if they're dead.' Teresa was always so direct.

'I know. They're just not there for me. I feel like Tantalus – hungry and thirsty, but with the grapes and water all just out of reach. Rachel, Eduardo and Lucas are there – but they're not there. I'm going to miss out on so much.'

At least I now felt able to show my feelings – my sadness, my vulnerability . . . my sense of loss. And doing that seemed to ease the pain.

Teresa tried to reassure me. 'Mum will buy you a plane ticket so you can visit them.'

'And then it's all the parting and pain again . . . when will it all end?'

'Oh Eliza,' Teresa yawned. 'Go to bed. Go and dream . . . '

'But dreams won't bring them back . . . '

And it was not escape that I sought. I finally wanted to rid myself of all emotional turmoil, and find the inner strength to cope with any occurrence I was faced with in life.

The idea of going to northern Italy was to bring together those from different countries who had been close to Guruji over the years. I felt I would gain inspiration from attending such a gathering. Roopa's family had a house in Livigno that was large enough to accommodate twenty of us so it was thought appropriate to meet there. While Guruji had been with us our attention had always been focused on him, so now it seemed important that we get to know each other better. Although there was an underlying bond between us owing to all the experiences that we had been through together, there were different ideas as to how Guruji's teachings should be passed on to others. I had often wondered how such an all-embracing philosophy could possibly be incorporated within an organizational structure.

Should it even be tried? But everyone seemed to agree that somehow we should make Guruji's meditation practices available to those who wanted them. The idea behind Livigno was not only to spend time with each other, but also to reach a common understanding as to the direction the meditation movement should go next.

The house was spacious and elegant, hemmed in by mountains that still had a thick covering of snow on them. As I looked out of the window towards the towering peaks, the place felt awesome, serving as a reminder that there would be no escape from here. While meditating together, the concentration of spiritual energy would intensify and, as in Cyprus, underlying tensions would be brought to the surface spontaneously. This would provide an opportunity for them to be released and dispersed.

As I looked around at the people present, I mused that no one could have guessed what interest we had in common. We seemed such a disparate collection of individuals – a cross-section of society. My own role was arbitrary. I realized that I was viewed with a certain amount of suspicion as I had been away from the movement for a while and I had no formal role within it. Also I had never had the chance of getting to know some of the newer teachers as, on the more recent courses, I had spent most of my time with Guruji. I now wanted to show my willingness to help in any way I could.

The first couple of days were spent meditating, chanting and sharing our ideas about various aspects of Guruji's teachings. Away from these times we shopped, cooked and socialized together. As time went by, however, it became apparent that feelings of unease were running deeper than any of us had initially realized. Maybe it was inevitable that they had to be directed somewhere . . . at someone . . . since Guruji was no longer there to absorb the tension. Allegations began to emerge. Roopa came to warn me: 'Usha, there are some derogatory things being said about you. I think you should know.'

'What kind of things?'

'Absurd things that have no truth in them. There are those here who don't know you. It seems that events from the past are being dredged up and used against you.'

'But what? There's nothing to dredge up . . . '

'Sujay and I were up until four in the morning trying to explain your position. But it appears weak if someone does that for another. You'll have to speak up for yourself, Usha.'

I realized that Roopa was trying to help me, but I did not know to what she was alluding. I acknowledged that my attempts to get on with those from different countries may have appeared trite, but I was not sure how people viewed the future of the movement and I decided it was safer to avoid sensitive subject matter. I wondered at my own vision: secretly I doubted that any structure could ever represent Guruji's ideals. When the mystics passed on, their words were all too often translated into religious beliefs and human frailty got in the way of Truth. Who of us really understood Guruji's teachings anyway? At this stage I was more inclined to think that his ideas would be carried forward by just a few individuals. But I was reluctant to express that view – it could have upset the present gathering and I would not have wanted to do that.

When we met as a group again, I watched people's comments and expressions more carefully and became aware that surreptitious arrows were being aimed in my direction. Roopa wrote me a note in large letters: USHA, IT'S TIME THAT YOU STOOD UP FOR YOURSELF. Then she spoke out: 'I think we need to clear up the 'Usha issue'. I sense that there are undercurrents stirring and these should be brought out into the open. If there is anyone who has concerns about Usha's position here, it's only right that she should hear them. At the very least she should be given the opportunity of explaining herself.'

There seemed to be a general consensus that this would be a good idea, and that evening was set aside for this purpose.

Roopa turned to me. 'How do you feel about it Usha? Do you mind?'

'No . . . I don't suppose so.' But I felt distinctly uncomfortable – I had no clear idea what the 'Usha issue' was all about.

Before the evening session I went upstairs to be quiet for a while. I was sharing a room with Sutriya and she suggested that we meditate together. When we opened our eyes, she looked at me serenely. 'Don't worry Usha – we're with you . . . '

I remembered the time in Cyprus when Guruji had brought Vidya, Roopa, Sutriya and me together to enhance the flow of energy between us. I had always felt close to the American teachers and I was aware that I needed their strength now. As I went out into the corridor I met Vidya; she approached me and placed her finger firmly on my forehead. 'That's Guruji's blessing.' The heat from her hand seared through me and I felt empowered by her touch. I was ready to go downstairs.

It had been arranged that the meeting should be chaired by someone who did not know me, so that neutrality would be maintained. Calmly I took my seat – 'the hot seat' as someone commented wryly.

The meeting began: 'We're all aware that there are feelings about Usha that need to be resolved. Tonight we hope we'll be able to do that. Shall I begin?'

Initially I thought it strange that the chairman should start the debate, but then there was nothing usual about that night. It was theatre of the macabre, and the play was about to start.

He addressed me formally. 'Usha, it seems that there is a conflict inside you . . . a psychological problem . . . ' My mouth dropped open in surprise – not just at the comment itself, but because it had been made by this supposedly 'neutral' chairman. What on earth did he mean? He continued: 'I am aware that you are married to John who has little interest in Guruji or the meditation process. He is a completely different type of character to you and this is bound to cause a disturbance within you . . .'

As he was talking, I became more and more dumb-founded by the ideas that he was putting forward. He had never met John, and hardly knew me. How could he presume so much? I concluded that he must have been talking from hearsay. When he had finished his piece, the next person began.

'You left the movement, Usha. Why did you leave?'

'You know why I left. I got married.'

'But your leaving could be interpreted differently . . . '

Of course it could: it could be interpreted in as many ways as there are people in this room – but *I* know why I left. This idea was elaborated on for a while but I had ceased to pay attention. All I was wondering was how on earth this had begun? I could understand that my reluctance to speak out had made me an unknown quantity – suspicions could easily arise. These were teachers who regarded it as their responsibility to protect and further Guruji's teachings, and clearly they saw me as a threat. Over the years there had been little stability in the movement owing to the constant flux of people who had come and gone. I had always presumed that this was due to the nature of Guruji's teachings themselves – namely that everyone should find their own path. But this recurring pattern had made it difficult to organize a stable structure through which such teachings could be transmitted to others. I recognized that there were problems.

Yet, there was a deeper thought inside me that was stirring too. As I sat there listening to these people's questions and assumptions, I realized that I doubted them just as much as they doubted me. I could see that we were all being drawn into the same game of assessing and judging one another – the difference was that they were expressing their views while I chose to remain silent. Why did I find it so difficult to speak out . . . to speak my mind? I wanted someone to defend me . . . to say something on my behalf – but this time I was being forced to stand alone.

I was jolted back from my meanderings when the next person began. 'Some years back we think that you may have been involved in trying to disrupt Guruji's teaching. You went to a meeting in 1980 . . . '

I interrupted. 'I never went to any meeting. I was married by then.'

'But we can get proof.'

Proof? What was this – a court of law? The insinuations went on and on.

'Usha, you're very charming on the surface but underneath . . . I suspect you may have ulterior motives.'

'What, may I ask?'

'I think you have illusions about your role within the

organization,' came the formal reply.

Then another voice. 'You're not as wise as you think you are Usha . . . '

What about you? I thought to myself, but again I was reluctant to speak out.

The innuendoes had become so bizarre that all I could now hear echoing through my mind was: Usha is . . . Usha is . . . Usha is . . . like a mantra. Usha is what? I thought to myself. Usha is nothing but a fabrication of these people's minds – in reality she is none of these things. Usha is Usha – someone who is struggling to find her True Self. All I became aware of were different versions of Usha being tossed from one end of the room to the other. Was this nothing but an extraordinary display of people's mental aberrations? I just happened to be sitting in the hot seat – the focal point.

Yet, through it all, I was being offered a profound insight into the nature of the human mind – my own included. Was this the barrier, so full of distortion, that prevented humankind from realizing its spiritual centre? Through our conditioned, limited and confused minds, we spontaneously judge each other and place ourselves in a better light. And I did the same. The more they fired off questions and voiced their suspicions, the more firmly I came to the conclusion that these people were controlling and vindictive. As they judged me, I judged them . . . and I could not stop myself from doing it. We were all being dragged down into this bottomless pit together, and the frightening realization was that this endless play for superiority goes on all the time amongst humankind . . . putting others down in order to raise ourselves up. It was the means of protecting our ego-self.

Roopa was trying to interrupt the proceedings: 'I think Usha should be given a chance to speak.'

From within me a clarity and power surfaced that at the time seemed to have little to do with me.

'I came to Livigno in gratitude for everything that Guruji has done for me. There's no point in trying to defend myself as there's nothing to defend. All I want to say is that I'm bewildered by the tone of what I'm hearing tonight. I've always believed that the more we understand ourselves, the better equipped we will be to help others. There are so many people out there desperately needing practical help in their daily lives . . . and that's what Guruji came to offer us. This all seems so far removed from anything that Guruji stood for. I don't believe that by judging each other we'll find the answers that we're looking for. We're here to *understand* each other. Surely we should be looking at ourselves, exploring the deeper levels of our being, our own feelings, to see what is preventing us from realizing our true nature – which is Love. That's what I want more of anyway.'

There was silence – and then the voices began again. Once more I tried to take the argument to a different level but I was getting tired. I had been there for almost two hours when Roopa interjected: 'I think it's time we took a break. We can resume later if we want.'

In the change of mood that came from having a drink and a walk around, I was approached by one or two of those who had challenged me.

'Well done, Usha . . . you're very strong, aren't you? Remember, whatever is said is just surface sparring – it's the underlying bond between us that matters. It enables us to be open with each other without holding resentment.'

But I did hold resentment – I felt threatened and afraid. I had been weakened by the projections that had been thrown at me. I reached for a cigarette; I had not smoked since I was at drama school. I knew that there was a lesson to be learned, but I could not see for the life of me what it was. Was this whole scenario being played out to test my strength or show me my weakness? Or was it to demonstrate that no organization or belief system could ever lead a person to ultimate freedom? Maybe I had to leave these people and find my own way? Yet, for some reason, that response did not ring true – it smacked of escapism and I had had enough of that. No. I wanted to find a way out of this predicament without turning my back on it. After all, this drama clearly brought out the positive and negative forces of life . . . and I wanted to learn to fly free within them.

I could see the battleground marked out in front of me: the opposing forces were lined up – the mind and the heart, reason and intuition, male and female. Balance was needed between the polarities – all the different elements had to come together in One. Had not Guruji always told us that peace was beyond understanding . . . beyond the mind? And we were still immersed in mind games. In a peculiar way I felt privileged at being offered this unique insight into the make-up of the human mind – Guruji symbolized an ideal that was so close to people's hearts that it tore away at us and exposed our dross.

During the brief moments when I was able to stand back from the play I saw us as puppets on a string. When each comment or remark was made, it was as though Guruji was urging us on to probe deeper within ourselves. But what was he trying to show *me*? What was this dark area within me that needed lightening? Tucked away among these mountains there were no distractions – we had come here to face ourselves and learn. Through being with one another, it was as though the processes of life were being accelerated just as they had been when Guruji was around. Now here – in the middle of nowhere – we were being challenged to know ourselves.

When I awoke the following morning, I felt fragile . . . I had been affected by the onslaught more than I had realized. I trembled at the thought of going downstairs. All I wanted now was for there to be peace between us all. I bathed, dressed in clean clothes, and made my way to the dining-room. There was a group of people sitting around the breakfast table and I approached them tentatively. My resolve to be strong was rapidly disappearing as I yearned for some consolation, a kind word . . . a little comfort. I wanted to make amends and for the conflict between us to cease.

I hesitated before I spoke. 'I'm sorry if I've done anything to upset you. I never meant to offend anyone. Please let's put all this behind us . . . I just want to work alongside you. I'm sorry all this has happened.'

I listened while the response rained down on me.

'Usha – you have a lesson to learn, and our job is to teach you.'

Yes. I did have a lesson to learn – and they were teaching me. I headed straight for the door aware that Madhu, one of the American teachers, was coming after me. She followed me back to my room and there she put her arm around me and whispered: 'Courage Usha, don't listen to them.' Relieved that she was with me, I collapsed on the bed exhausted, cradling my head in my hands.

When I looked up a few moments later, I noticed that Madhu had moved by the window. As she stood there, it seemed as though light was radiating through her. She then began to speak with such a clarity and calmness that I became transfixed by her presence.

'Usha, you're a beautiful soul and you must never forget that. Remember how Guruji loved you. You *must* find the courage to express who you truly are – that is your dharma. You will never find yourself by trying to please others. You're not meant to cower and live in fear. If you do you will be beaten down again and again. You have to live in your own truth. That's what Guruji has been trying to teach you all these years . . . and that's what he's telling you now. For as long as you deny yourself, you will suffer inside. It's been your nature for so long. This pattern has to be broken and here, amongst these people, you have the opportunity to do that. Take it – be brave. You have to begin to stand in your own truth. This is the path of Self-realization.'

I wanted to tell her how much I had appreciated her insight and caring, but I was too dazed by the realizations that were flooding through my mind. All my life I had found it easier to do what others expected of me rather than be myself. Had this framework not been in place since childhood? For so long I had shrunk from conflict and controversy believing it easier to remain silent. But I was beginning to feel suffocated. Here in Livigno – thank God – I had been pushed up against the wall so hard that I had been forced to see this part of myself that I had justified for so long. How had my mask of self-righteousness so effectively concealed my mine-field of underlying fear?

Later that morning, after the windows had been opened to let in fresh air, Roopa suggested that we conclude the previous evening by each of us saying what we had learned from it. When it came to my turn, I felt lucid and clear.

'If I were to please each one of you, I would have to take on as many personalities as there are people in this room. And even then I don't believe that any of you would be satisfied. It would be foolish of me to even try. I realize that I have to be myself – to say what I think and to express who I am – in other words be me. Whatever the consequences of that decision, I am prepared to accept them. You can take me or leave me as I am.'

As I spoke the words, feelings of elation washed through me. In that moment I no longer cared how I was seen by the rest of the world . . . at last I felt free to be me.

There was a sauna in the basement of the house which the Spaniards liked to use. I decided to join them. I thought it would help me get rid of some of the clag from my system. As we sat together on the pine boards, absorbing the steamy atmosphere, I enjoyed the intimacy of our surroundings and gradually began to unwind.

Ramón, a teacher from Madrid, looked across and smiled at me. 'Usha, what was all that about last night? I didn't understand any of it.'

'I'm not sure I did either,' I replied. 'It was probably different for us all. For me an old trait of mine was pushed right in front of my nose. I want it resolved and last night may have helped me to do that. It's too easy to avoid facing oneself . . . we've perfected the art.'

Ramón became thoughtful. 'Transformation is a painful process – but once we begin it, it seems that we get carried along by a force that's much greater than us. Sometimes I find it frightening.'

An image came into my mind. 'It's as though we're like drops of water in a mountain stream which gathers more speed as it nears the ocean.'

'I think we deserve medals for what we put ourselves through,' he said smiling at me reassuringly. 'But the Spanish find it easier than the English you know.'

'Oh yes – why?' I said with a touch of sarcasm in my voice.

'Because we're more open . . . more passionate than you are. We allow ourselves to feel more and to express those feelings . . . because of that we find out what's going on inside.'

'Maybe I should come to Spain . . . '

Indeed – why did I persist in burying so much? How many times had I been shown this pattern before? That true courage is not a show of bravado or independence, not a fake subservience or a silent suffering. No. It is the ability to be oneself without any façade or superficiality. How well I knew the damage that could be caused by putting a lid on one's emotions – and usually it was only done to make others feel comfortable. We end up protecting others as a way of protecting oneself from any negativity that might rebound on us.

In Livigno I had not been allowed to play the role of victim . . . the game which ensures that sympathy and kindness are received. I was glad. I no longer wanted to suffer the humiliation of seeking love from others – it was time that I became so filled up with it that I could only offer it instead. My initial resentment against those who had spoken out dissolved quickly, and was replaced instead by a deep sense of gratitude for their directness. It had allowed me to see traits in myself that had imprisoned me for years.

I was beginning to understand that there were three aspects to Guruji's teaching: firstly there was Guruji, the mystic and teacher himself. Secondly, there were his teachings transmitted through both his words and deeds and, thirdly, there was his family of devoted meditators or *chelas*. It was this *chela-body* that I likened to families all over the world, in that it was made up of so many differences of character and opinion that spirited argument became inevitable. But it was through such interaction that we now had the opportunity of learning more about ourselves. Since Guruji was gone, we had to be a mirror for each other. I had heard Roopa likening this to the Buddhist system, in which there is the Buddha or Enlightened One, then the *Dharma* or Way, and lastly the *Sangha* – those who come together to embrace and follow the teachings.

I recognized that our time together in Livigno had been the play of karma, in which we all had the opportunity to grow. Each one of us faced our own mountain to climb, and I knew that others had found it as painful a process as I had. Knots within us that may have constricted us for years, had been untied and released. And no taste of bitterness was left to linger. By the time we left for our different destinations, the mountain air had blown away the dross, and the underlying bond between us had been significantly strengthened.

On my way home I wondered how any spiritual organization could possibly assist individuals with the process of unfoldment. It seemed that all that could be done was to offer people the tools, or techniques, to perform the task themselves. Spiritual flowering is a process of liberation which could so easily be thwarted by rules and regulations. No one held the same view. Beliefs had to be allowed to change as vision expanded – and there lay the paradox. Guidelines were necessary for social beings to live together harmoniously, yet dogma and rigidity led to judgment and division. No wonder so much confusion reigned within religions. Strong opinions constrained the mind instead of allowing it to open up, as so many people had experienced within different religions throughout time.

Spirituality was the ability to live life to the full with no holding back – just an opening of oneself to One Self. Surely the only way such an experience could be initiated in another was through openness, love and understanding. Yes. To become truly free one had to go beyond all opinions, judgments, beliefs and views – in other words to transcend all form.

From such spiritual adventures and realizations, it was with relief that I returned to John, the children, the fells and dales. Home was my source of comfort. It was here that I could relax with the family, enjoy the company of my friends and dream up new projects. Within the security of that environment, I was able to put into practice the lessons that I had learned through my spiritual encounters. From Dent I was able to push boundaries further, challenge myself deeper, and discover in what direction I should go next.

From Cambridge, to London and on to the northern hills, my outer environment had always seemed to reflect the changes that were taking place inside me at the time. Maybe it was for this reason that I now felt pulled so strongly towards a group of remote and unspoiled islands in the middle of the Indian Ocean – namely the Seychelles. To me this place represented an ideal within the physical world – and it was this ideal that I now sought within myself.

On the back of the success of one of our shepherding books, we had taken Charlotte to these islands on our first and only holiday together for nine years. I had been captivated, not just by the beauty of the landscape, but by the carefree nature of the people who lived there. Always in search of new photographic opportunities, John and I had been drawn to the idea of documenting the lives of the in-shore fishermen. We were used to working alongside those who lived close to nature, and we mused that fishermen would make a welcome change from the hill farmers that we were used to. As a result, as soon as we returned home from our holiday adventure, we began looking for sponsorship so that we could plan a proper photographic trip. It was not long before we had found a sympathetic ear.

As with our previous projects we determined to cover the story as comprehensively as possible. In this case we wanted to be able to photograph beneath the sea as well as above it, so that we could record the effects that the local fishing had on the coral reef. It was with this specific intention in mind that we decided to take an intensive scuba-diving course. I had always felt at home in the water so learning the new techniques did not worry me. The first sessions were taught in a swimming pool, while the final open-water test was to take place at Coniston Water in the Lake District.

It was a November day and there were snow flurries and a bitter wind blowing. I began to feel nervous as we drove to the appointed place.

'Dry suits are essential for a day like this. You'd get too cold in wet suits.'

This all seemed very far removed from photographing the wonders of reef life in warm tropical waters. The business of kitting up reminded me of past caving trips, though this time we also had the extra burden of carrying heavy air bottles to the lake shore.

'Now, take your time as you descend. There's a level area about forty feet down – we'll go through the different skills there.'

It was a grim place. The water was murky and there was nothing to see but stones and silt on the bottom. My ears hurt on the way down, so I went slowly to give time for the pressure to readjust. For the first test we had to take our air-line out of our mouth, let it go, and then relocate and replace it. Clearly it was an important procedure to accomplish efficiently as, literally, our lives depended on it.

I watched the others complete the task successfully and awaited my turn. I felt calm, even though I was already beginning to feel cold. Then I took the regulator out of my mouth and let the air-line float off behind me. As I had done in the pool, I swung my arm back to retrieve it. But this time I did not feel it land across my shoulder. Unconcerned I tried again . . . but still it was not there. I could feel the panic beginning to rise. I had to get air soon – already this had taken too long. Back again I swung my arm determined to get my line . . . but still nothing landed over my shoulder. The only thought that filled my mind was that I had no air and time was running out. In desperation I looked at my instructor, using my eyes to implore him for help. As I stared at him, the solution came: he was kneeling directly in front of me with his regulator in his mouth. Of course . . . I could just take his. I lunged forward to grab his mouth-piece but, before I could reach it, he put his arm out to stop me. Calmly he showed me that my own air-line had been lying across my shoulder all along. I simply had not felt it through the thickness of my dry suit.

I was thrown – shocked by the experience. My behaviour had been involuntary and I had witnessed a part of myself that I had not seen before. My instinct had been to take someone else's air. Ridden with guilt and feeling increasingly nervous, I proceeded with the other tests. When we had finished, we made our controlled ascent to the surface. I exploded with apologies. 'I'm so sorry. How could I have done such a thing? I panicked and tried to take your air . . . I can't believe it. I didn't know I was capable of doing such a thing.'

'Don't worry about it,' my instructor reassured me. 'Come on, let's go and have some coffee and warm up before this afternoon's session.'

Did I have to go on? Did I have to go back down to that God-forsaken place and take the regulator out of my mouth again? I was now shaking with cold as well as fear. Not only did I quickly have to come to terms with the awfulness of what I had done, but I also had to face going through the whole thing again. The instructor's voice broke into my confusion. 'Eliza, this afternoon's test isn't difficult. All you have to do is to come to the surface while sharing air with John. If you have any problems just signal, and remember – take your time. Now let's get on with it before we get any colder.'

Because I was slight, I was shivering more than the others. We warmed our hands by pouring hot water into our gloves and then headed back to the shore. All I had to say was 'no' – but, like a zombie, I found myself going through the same procedure all over again. Once more my ears hurt on the way down, and again I was frightened when I reached the bottom. Then all at once I found myself facing John, mentally preparing myself for the exercise.

I told myself that all I had to do was pass the air back and forth while ascending to the surface. It was a safety procedure in case someone ran out of air. Before we began I drew a deep breath, concerned that something might go wrong. Then I took out my mouth-piece and signalled to John that I was out of air. He handed me his. Maybe it was because my face was so cold, or perhaps it was because there was so much fear inside me . . . whatever it was, I simply could not get his regulator into my mouth.

There was only one place to go and that was up. All I could

216

think of was the vastness of the sky with all that air. Down in those murky depths, there was none. All rational thought vanished as panic took over. I threw aside mouth pieces, air-lines, helping arms, and went for the surface. I was not going to die down there. My attention was focused only upward . . . toward the light. And yet the ripples on the surface seemed so far away. I thought that I would never make it, that I had embarked upon an impossible feat. I felt as though I was suffocating . . . was this what drowning was like? There was no breath, no energy left in me to go on. In one last act of desperation, I thrashed wildly with my arms and legs in an attempt to get more propulsion . . . and then at last I broke the surface. I gasped and gasped again for air but I could not get it inside me. My airways must have all closed up.

I was aware of a commotion around me as the instructor pulled me towards the shore. 'She's come up nearly forty feet . . . we'll have to get her to hospital. At least I managed to punch her in the chest to make sure she breathed out on the way up.'

The pain started that evening – first in my ears, then in my neck and shoulders. The doctor suggested that I might have picked up an infection and prescribed antibiotics and pain-killers. But it got worse. 'It feels as though there's a bolt right through my neck,' I attempted to explain to John.

On the third evening the pain grew so intense that John insisted on calling the doctor again. 'Just increase the pain-killers. The muscles in the neck have all gone into spasm.'

As soon as I heard that I called David, an osteopath, who had helped me once before. He gave me an appointment for the following day.

'You're very blocked up,' he commented. 'What have you been up to?'

'A diving accident.'

As he examined me, he said quietly: 'You've gone inside yourself, Eliza.'

Are you surprised, I thought to myself? And chose not to reply.

We sank into silence as he moved his hands from neck to head and back again, releasing the tension in an extraordinarily gentle way. At the end of the session he instructed me firmly but kindly: 'Now go straight home to bed . . . you need rest. Come again the day after tomorrow. I don't think you'll need those pills any more.'

He was right. I was more comfortable with the idea of releasing tension rather than suppressing it, so the pills were put to one side. After a couple more sessions, the pain had gone and I had the movement back in my neck again. But something else had happened too. As my neck freed itself, my mind did likewise. Each day that went by, I saw the world and myself in a different way.

Maybe I had to go down to those murky depths in order to pierce the veils and see more clearly? For so long I had pretended to be something I was not . . . to be 'a good, brave girl'. Indeed I had worked so hard to maintain that image. Why did I almost have to drown myself before realizing its absurdity? I had panicked at the first upset – that was not brave. I had tried to take someone's else's air – that was certainly not good. No. I was neither of those things. Both episodes had succeeded in exploding my act in my face. And it was such a relief! Such a heavy weight had been lifted from my shoulders and it made me feel so much lighter.

All at once I had become ordinary in my own eyes . . . capable of being weak, afraid, and of performing the most terrible of acts. I was not a saint but a sinner; and to realize that made me feel so utterly human, so much more in touch with other people, with their frailties and fears. How could I ever judge or blame another now? It was as though my defences had come tumbling down in one fell swoop and exposed all the façades that I had hidden behind all these years. At last I had been made to undress – and the nakedness felt good.

A few weeks later I met Mario, one of the Spanish teachers, who had come to a course in England. I told him the story of my diving accident.

His eyes lit up. 'Do you remember the story that Ramakrishna told? He said that's how much someone has to want God . . . like a drowning man wants air.'

'Oh no, I'm not sure I'll ever want God that much!' I exclaimed. 'It's too much like hard work. First we have to let go of our attachments, then our beliefs, and finally strip off naked. What are we doing it all for?'

'Nothing, I suppose.'

I smiled at his response. 'It's funny isn't it? Here we all are busy striving towards nothingness.'

'But there's everything in the nothingness, Usha.'

'And the experience comes when we're ready for it. Meanwhile . . . life puts us through its paces.'

'Hello. Is that Mrs Forder?'

'Yes, can I help?'

'I'm from medical insurance. There's nothing to be concerned about, but I'm afraid to tell you that your father had a mild heart-attack yesterday. He's at present in hospital in Ajaccio.'

My father had gone to Corsica on a botanical trip. We all admired his determination in pursuing such ventures when he was over eighty; but this time we had been concerned as the day before his departure he had complained of chest pains. The doctor, however, had assured us that it was just an old stomach problem playing up, probably due to nerves about the journey. Maybe news of the attack should not have surprised me but, nevertheless, anxiously I fired questions at the man at the end of the phone.

'Will he be alright? Does my mother know? When did it happen?'

'Your father's comfortable at present but he has to remain very quiet. The trouble is that we can't locate your mother. Do you know where she is?'

'I think she's away on a parliamentary visit. I'll find out and get her to call you at once.'

Like my father, my mother had the energy of a young woman, tirelessly committing herself to environmental and educational reforms, while still enjoying an active social life herself. Within hours I had managed to track her down and she booked herself on the first flight to Corsica. Both my brothers now lived in Canada but fortunately Nic was on sabbatical and staying at the family home in Cornwall. We all kept in close touch during the following days. One message was relayed after another to say how my father was doing, whether he had managed to eat anything, if he had done any reading, and how often he had been able to see my mother during the day. Above all, we were told, he needed rest. Apparently my father had insisted from his sick bed that on no account were we to postpone or cancel our trip to the Seychelles. But I felt hesitant about going away when he was so ill, and John and I decided to put back our departure by a couple of weeks anyway.

It was four days after the initial attack that I called Nic for a further report. 'Did you talk to Mum last night? How's the patient?' I asked cheerily. Everything seemed to be going well, and we had been informed that it would soon be safe for him to fly home.

'I've just heard. He had another massive attack early this morning.'

I was astounded. What did it mean? Was there still a chance, some hope?

'I don't understand. What are you saying?' I asked filled with trepidation.

'I'm flying out there. I'll phone Sebastian – you let Teresa know.'

'So that's it isn't it? That's what you're saying. It's over, isn't it?'

'It looks like it. But that's how he would have wanted it . . . '

Another loss. Another parting. But this time there had been no chance to say goodbye . . . I pictured the rugged handsome face of my father in my mind as I tried to readjust to the news. His presence was with me so powerfully.

As soon as my mother and Nic returned from Corsica, the rest of us congregated in Cambridge and the family was brought together for the first time in over thirty years. The sense of unity gave us comfort and we supported my mother in every way we could. We buoyed up her spirits, as her strength lifted ours. Just one night had she spent alone, in a strange hotel in a foreign country, coming to terms with her husband's death, while waiting for my brother to arrive. At least he had been there to cope with the strange funeral parlours hung heavy with dark red drapes. They had been asked what clothes my father should be laid out in, and in their broken French they had had to explain that they wanted no clothes in particular. 'I hope they put a drape around him and didn't take us literally!'

My mother's courage and dignity touched us all in a profound way. We laughed, and then cried, as my brothers rehearsed a John Donne poem and a passage from Corinthians that they were to read at the funeral. Excerpts from Elgar, Schubert and Bach were chosen to reflect my father's greatest passion of all. Grandchildren arrived from different parts of Britain and Europe to say goodbye to a man whom they had all loved and respected deeply. But Rachel was missing. She lit candles and celebrated my father's life and death alone in Argentina. He had always adored her.

My mother asked me to organize the flowers and I felt privileged to do so. I took the children to see Faith, a close friend of my parents, who had a large, beautiful and wild garden. Together we picked branches from flowering shrubs and trees, selected different patterned foliage, searched the borders and vegetable gardens for an array of colour, and between us carried back armfuls of greenery to the house. There Faith boldly made the first move by sticking a three-foot-high branch into one of the oases that she had bought. From that point on there was no holding back. His coffin was destined to look like her garden – vibrant, colourful and full of untamed beauty.

John sat on one side of me and Teresa on the other. I could not take my eyes off my father's coffin. Flowers and leaves cascaded from it in abundance. It was so full of life and hope. Gururaj's word came to my mind: There is no death . . . only life. Tears flowed down my cheeks – there was no stopping them. To the evocative sounds of the piano impromptu, feelings washed through me that seemed to cleanse and heal. I was overcome by an exquisite, liquid, boundless love that seemed to permeate my whole being and radiate out towards my father and all those present. There was no hurt or pain, not even a feeling of loss, just an extraordinarily powerful emission of love for a great man. Together we were there to celebrate his life – yet the qualities expressed through my father were eternal. His death could not interrupt their flow.

That evening, as my mother sat at the dinner table with her children and grandchildren around her, I could not take my eyes off her. She was dressed in a blue suit which was set off by the gold of her necklace. The colours complemented the grey-white of her hair. She looked regal and graceful . . . even if a little forlorn. A radiance emanated from her and I felt moved and proud. She appeared as 'mother' to so much more than her offspring. Throughout her life she had always concerned herself with the welfare of her family, friends and colleagues, and increasingly her capacity for compassion and caring had become an intrinsic part of her nature. The role of giver suited her.

Drawn by her presence, I looked more deeply within her. It was as though my father's qualities were now imbibed in her. All at once I felt like a child again, humble and full of awe, sitting at the feet of my father and mother.

Life is a succession of emergences.

Just as a snake sheds its skin, we have to shed our past over and over again . . . until finally we are set free.

10

Idid not want to leave my mother but I had little choice. We had already postponed our flight to the Seychelles and we were now due to leave the following day.

So, from that thin line which divides life and death, John and I flew off to a place once known as the forgotten Eden – a group of islands four degrees south of the equator and a thousand miles from the nearest mainland. When we arrived I was not only dazed by the emotional trauma of the past few days, but I was tired from the flight, and unused to the oppressive humidity that greeted us as we got off the plane. 'I need time before I pick up a camera, John.'

He encouraged me to rest for a couple of days, while he went off to find out about hiring scuba-gear so that he could begin on some underwater photography. I took a bus north to a small village where we had spent some days on our previous trip. I wanted to immerse myself in the warm tropical waters, absorb the sun's heat, and regain my energy again. I sat in the shade under the palm trees, let the sand trickle through my fingers, and looked out to sea to where some fishermen were pulling in their nets. No tourists were about: there hardly ever were in this place so far away from anywhere. After a little while I wandered across to where some older men were playing dominoes.

'Do you know if Herman is about?' I asked tentatively.

It was two years since we had last been there. Maybe he had moved on.

'Herman? He is out there. See.' And one of them pointed to

the fishing boats.

'Is he helping with the nets?'

'Yes. He will come shortly.'

I returned to the beach to enjoy the spectacle of this distant figure, silhouetted against the sun, diving down and reappearing somewhere else, freeing the nets as he did so. I had forgotten how magical this place was. After half an hour or so I noticed that Herman was swimming directly towards me. Although the shore was half a mile or so long, it appeared that he was heading exactly for the place where I sat. Momentarily I grew apprehensive, wondering if he would remember me. Like an ocean creature he emerged from the sea with two octopus threaded on his stick. He had a strong stocky body, no doubt gained from all the swimming he did. His dreadlocks were more bleached by the sun than I had remembered.

'Herman?' I said, squinting at him against the sun.

'Eliza? Is it you?'

I went towards him. 'I can't believe we are together again. How are you?'

'It is you, Eliza. You are really here. While I was swimming I saw a woman with a camera and I began thinking of you. Where is John and Charlotte?'

'Charlotte's not here, but John is. He's finding out about scuba-diving.'

'You must both come for a beer tonight . . . about six o'clock. It's OK?'

'We'll be there.'

That evening John and I returned to sit under the trees with Herman and his friends. We exchanged news while watching the sun sink behind the ribbons of cloud that had gathered over Silhouette Island. I was reminded of how quickly the sun sets in the tropics and noted that we should remember that when we photographed. We told Herman of our plans and he suggested that we stay at a friend's house to make our living costs cheaper. He also offered to act as our guide, which would enable us get to know people and places quicker.

Herman never carried money but bartered the one or two

octopus that he caught by day for essential provisions; otherwise he lived off fish from the sea and fruit from the trees. Each morning he would bring us a gift – a mango, bananas, breadfruit, and sometimes a few eggs when he knew we were tired of eating fish. In Herman we discovered a friend who displayed such warmth and generosity that we knew our time in Seychelles was going to be infinitely richer for our meeting. He was someone who owned nothing, but offered everything.

So, in this faraway idyll, an adventure began in which I was to find a freedom I had not known before. Physically, I was rid of my clothes, emotionally I had no responsibility, mentally there was no pressure to meet any deadline, and spiritually I experienced an unparalleled sense of joy. While relating to the local people, there was such a sense of ease, that it seemed as though life was a continual celebration of living and being together. On a whim we could immerse ourselves in the tropical seas, and the physical exertion of walking along forest paths and cliff-tops to the wilder places on the islands, I found energising. Never before had I had so much time to watch the play of light on the sea and the sand, or to study the obscure shapes of the large granite boulders that served as a backdrop to the miles of empty beach. Nor had I had the opportunity to observe in such close detail the flora that covered the islands, and the animals and birds that inhabited them. At last I had found a space in my life in which I could become totally absorbed in nature.

From one island we ventured to the next, photographing the landscape, people and the wildlife and showing how the three interacted with each other. When we returned to the main island, Herman was there to welcome us. He greeted us with some shells that he had found for Charlotte.

'Are you going octopus-fishing tomorrow? We'd like to photograph you at work.'

'It'll be a good day for it,' agreed Herman. 'The sea is calm.'

We arranged that John would use scuba-gear while I would snorkel alongside Herman and help relay messages. I watched

Herman as he swam just ahead of me, his fins steadily pumping away at the water to propel himself along. He seemed so much a part of the ocean. He showed me the reef in a way that I had not seen it before, as a living organism in which each part is intricately woven into the whole. He encouraged me to dive deep so that I could see close up the distinctive colours of fish I had never seen before, and the subtly of the different corals that grew. Alongside Herman I had no fear – the waters were warm, I felt confident and relaxed, and I had an inspirational guide who wanted me to experience the underwater world as he did.

I was startled by the sound of sudden splashing and Herman's voice shouting out excitedly. 'Look Eliza – an octopus.' He pointed downward with his finger.

'Where?' I looked but could see nothing. Later I found out that it takes an expert's eye to locate them.

'There. I show you.' And down he went.

I dived after him and watched as he prised the octopus out of its hole and pierced it through with his stick. The black ink spurted out defiantly into the ocean. Then together we combined the ingredients of fisherman, water and light in differing ways to capture the scene on film. In that extraordinarily beautiful environment, with the sun's rays highlighting the reef through the water, our work became play . . . a dance of creation.

One day Herman would not go fishing. 'It's Corpus Christi.'

'What does that mean?'

'It means that we can't fish.'

'What happens if you do?'

'God won't be pleased.'

'And what happens when He's not pleased?' I asked with curiosity.

'He might send a shark to get me.'

'Oh Herman!' I exclaimed.

'I take a holiday instead,' he smiled.

'Don't you go to church?'

'No.'

'But Herman, you're afraid to go fishing because God might be angry, yet you don't go to church. Where's the sense?' I was curious to find out more about his beliefs.

'I don't know.'

'Would you take me to church?'

'Yes.'

By that time we had a large audience enjoying our repartee and everyone wanted to join in: 'But if Herman goes to church, the roof might fall in!'

Bets were laid on whether Herman would appear the following morning to accompany me to the first service of the day. To my surprise, he arrived promptly in the new shorts and T-shirt that John and I had bought him as a birthday present. Together we walked down the street to the cheers and jeers from his friends. He waved back at them smiling, undeterred by the attention that we were receiving.

I decided to confide in him. 'Herman, you should know that I've never been to mass.'

'Do not worry. I'll tell you what to do. When you go in, you take some water and go like this.' And he made the sign of the cross. Then he went on to explain. 'I only go to mass at Christmas, so today God will be pleased with both of us.'

'Does that mean more octopus?'

'It means that we will be looked after.'

'I'm glad of that,' I murmured quietly. 'Life's so simple for you, isn't it Herman?'

But he had no time to respond; we had arrived at the church.

On our last night, as a celebration of our time there, Herman offered to cook us a variety of local fish dishes. We invited our new friends to the occasion, and music was laid on and beer brought in. We ate, danced and told stories late into the night. It was not until most of the guests had left that the reality of our imminent departure hit home.

'I don't want you to go.' Herman said quietly.

'Don't Herman. I hate these partings . . . I've been through them before.'

'I will cry.' He said unabashed.

'So will I.'

'You see?' He said quietly, 'Life's not so simple. I get sad sometimes.'

'Herman, I've spent all my life realizing how important it is to be oneself. You are that – you have no pretensions. But just now I think we should pretend . . . pretend that we will see each other again soon. It'll make parting easier. Either you come to England, or we will come back here. '

'I'd like to come to England.'

'But it's so beautiful here in Seychelles . . . I don't want to leave these islands.'

'Is England far away . . . further than Bird Island?'

'Much, much further. You have to imagine us among hills and snow, and we'll think of you here.'

'I have a good imagination. And I dream . . . '

'I dream too . . . look at the night sky, Herman. We see the same stars from England. Whenever we look up at the stars, we'll think of each other.'

'I will always remember you.'

'As I will you. I've learned so much from you.'

'What things?' He asked in surprise. 'I cannot read or write.'

'About giving and loving . . . those sort of things.'

'But that's life.'

'Yes, but few know it, Herman. You own nothing, but offer everything – that's the art of life.'

As I sat in the airport lounge watching our plane being prepared for departure, strange feelings came over me. The act of going home seemed to have more import than just a return from a five-week adventure. I looked forward to seeing the children and Dent again, but I was leaving behind an experience that had been so liberating, that I was wondering whether I would ever be able to reclaim it. There was both sadness and happiness jostling around inside me, and I watched the feelings alternate, entwine and play alongside each other.

'How are you feeling?' Asked John, sensing my withdrawal.

'I'm not sure. I'm sad at leaving . . . but that's not surprising since I've never known such freedom before – but I'm also apprehensive about the future. I think that life's going to be different from now on.'

'How so?' John seemed puzzled.

'Guruji has gone . . . and now my father. To me they represent the spiritual and physical planes of existence. All that strength, goodness and humanity are no longer with us – yet their spirit lives on and somehow needs to be carried through in some way. Guruji's teaching is unique: he's a mystic of our time who has come to help ordinary people like you and me realize the True nature of the Self. By doing so, we discover the *extra-ordinariness* of life. Their deaths make me feel responsible . . . maybe that's why I feel apprehensive at the thought of going home.'

'You think too much Eliza, that's your trouble. I'll tell you a secret . . . '

'Go on then.'

John replied with gusto: 'The secret of life is to *live*.'

'But what happens when obstacles get in the way?'

'What sort of obstacles?' John seemed bewildered by my question.

'What are you afraid of, John?' I asked curiously.

'Flooded caves.'

I smiled. 'Typical – you always associate fear with physical danger. To me, fears are those tensions that affect us on a daily basis . . . insecurities that insidiously eat away at our lives. When we are rid of them . . . ah yes, then we are free to live. I think that the secret of life is to let go.'

'But if you let go, you fall.'

'And then you may die.' I said quickly. 'But it's better to die when you're still alive, as then you're free when the body goes. True dying is the conscious shedding of all our outer layers – the ultimate experience of nakedness. That's what Guruji tried to show me before he died. When you let go of everything, there's nothing left to tie you down. You're free to be anything and to merge with everyone. Imagine a world filled with that experience. We would care for each other as though the other was oneself.'

'I say live and you say die . . . who's right *then*?' John challenged me.

'The Zen paradox – the opposites are both true. Look at you and me.'

Not long after our return, a handful of British meditation teachers came together in an Indian restaurant to mull over our responsibilities regarding our way forward. I went along in search of inspiration. Despite conflicting ideas within different countries in the past, a calm was now settling. There was a general acceptance that everyone would always have their own views, but that these were just ripples on the surface of the pond. It was the underlying experience that mattered more.

'Do you know that we're the only meditation movement that's not banned by the Christians?' Tony informed us.

'Why's that?' We asked in surprise.

'Because they don't know about us.'

We collapsed in laughter. 'Is that a measure of our success?' I asked.

'Maybe it is,' Jaish mused. He had helped keep the British movement going over the years. 'At least we can't be accused of foisting beliefs on anyone. Guruji would be proud of us – we offer experience and that's all.'

Despite Christa's initial scepticism, she had now become a teacher and was busy expanding the group of meditators in Lancaster. Over the years we had spent many hours sharing ideas and listening to one other. She spoke thoughtfully: 'Sometimes I don't know what I'm doing. Why am I teaching something that I don't understand about myself?'

'It's that quality of not-knowingness that makes you such a good teacher, Christa. You are you – and that's why people are drawn to you.'

Jaish smiled. 'It's funny, isn't it? Here we all are feeling that we've gained so much, yet admitting that we don't know anything, aren't sure of what we should be doing or where we should be going.'

'And it doesn't matter.' Peter interjected. 'I think it's all much simpler than we realize.' He had been at Guruji's first talk in England and had been teaching ever since: he was now in his mid-seventies.

The conversation was interrupted by the waiter bringing us a selection of bhajis, curries, dahl and naan. While setting out our plates, one of them slipped.

Tony teased him: 'Meditation brings about balance you know?'

The Indian waiter gave a broad smile. 'What kind?'

'A kind I doubt you'll have heard of . . . ' The waiter seemed intrigued and left us to eat our meal.

'Times like this remind me of being with Guruji,' I reminisced.

'Except that now we can enjoy a meal in peace, without worrying about whether we're going to be thrown out of a restaurant,' Tony reminded us.

'True. But we had such fun . . . '

'And the fun took away the pain . . . at least some of it,' Lysney added thoughtfully.

The conversation prompted me to recount a recent dream. 'It was about Guruji. I was sitting next to him in a hall in South Africa that was filled with people. I leaned over towards him and whispered: "Tell me what it's like to be enlightened . . . I've been searching for so long." I looked at him and waited for a reply. Then, from behind me, I was aware of some movement in the hall. I turned around and saw that one by one all the people were leaving, without saying a word. I looked back at Guruji. At first I didn't understand what was happening, but then I realized that he was answering my question through the action that was taking place. Again I looked at the emptying hall, and then back at Guruji. He had become a shadow of himself. I spoke quietly, afraid that he would disappear completely. "Is freedom a state of being when you don't need anyone else . . . when you have everything that you need inside?" And the shadow of Guruji nodded.'

'That's it . . . I think Divinity has everything in hand,' Jaish concluded.

Lynsey interrupted, ' . . . not even in hand. Divinity just *is*.'

'Of course . . . the rain, the meal, us sitting here together, the interplay . . . it's all so perfect.' And I became lost in my own thoughts.

As we were leaving the restaurant, our waiter approached us. 'I'd like to know more about meditation.'

Peter turned to me. 'Why don't you tell him, Usha?'

'But it's such a long a story . . . I wouldn't know where to begin.'

Tony slipped him some information and – in that liberating state of not-knowingness – we departed.

It had become an annual event for Teresa's family and ours to meet up in Cornwall at the end of each summer. The children, mostly grown-up now, bring their friends along which means that there are enough of us to share the cooking, play cricket on the beach and take part in the ritual surfing marathons. When the weather is inclement we go for walks and talk.

A few of us were making our way along the cliff to a point where the rugged splendour of the Cornish coastline can be seen at its best. Occasionally I would move closer to the edge so that I could get a better look at the sheer rock face that plunged down to the sea two hundred feet below. Even though the sea was rough, the waves and billowing spray did not appear threatening from this height. Teresa's youngest son, Sam, had gone on in front. On the rocky outcrop ahead we could see his tall figure, dressed in black and topped with dark curls, silhouetted against the skyline. Standing on the promontory, he appeared like a director of a play. When we caught up with him, we sat together in a row and stared out to sea, mesmerized by the light that was playing on the water. How often we had done this over the years . . .

A flash of white suddenly caught my eye. 'Gannets – can you see them? They'll have been blown in by the off-shore winds.'

Far out, a couple of them were coasting along above the waves, their distinctive wings picked out by light.

As we watched them, I mused: 'They're the masters of the ocean, don't you think? I'd like to be one for a while . . . '

'I'd sooner be a panther – sleek, strong and fast,' said Sam.

'. . . but I don't think I'm seen quite like that.'

'How do we see you, Sam?'

'More like a grizzly bear . . . '

We burst out laughing at this vision of himself. Then I added my piece: 'I think I'm seen as a squirrel . . . all the time busying myself gathering nuts for the winter stores.'

'Worrying about your home and children, yea?'

'That's me.'

'Actually, I reckon there's a bit of the nun in you, Eliza,' Teresa said with a hint of sarcasm in her voice.

'If there's nun in me, there's too much in you!' I teased her back. By nature she had always been boisterous.

'I'd like to be a bat,' said John matter-of-factly.

'So you can live in your caves.'

'A large cave with a big river running through it . . . '

'I think I'll be a unicorn . . . then I can disappear and reappear without anyone knowing,' Abigail piped up unexpectedly.

We smiled at the different images of ourselves while we watched the storm clouds gathering on the horizon. A small fishing boat was heading out to sea. I broke the silence. 'Just imagine sailing off into that. It looks so dark and threatening out there. And the outcome is always unknown . . . '

'They'll be off for days,' said Teresa getting to her feet. 'Come on. Let's go before the rain starts. It's my turn to cook tonight and I want to buy some spices before the shops close.'

'I'll see you later.' And I left the family party to go back across the rocks. It was one of my favourite walks.

The wind was getting up, and I could feel the spray brushing against my cheeks the closer I got to the sea. Shafts of evening sunlight picked out the white tops of the waves that rode across the ocean as far as the eye could see. I chose my route carefully so as to avoid the deep, clear rock pools where my father and brothers had crabbed at low tide. Cornwall always reminded me of the good times in childhood. As I looked around for a smooth rock to sit on, I noticed how the barnacles glistened with water-droplets as they were left exposed by the out-going tide. A flock of oyster-catchers waited expectantly nearby, so I sat down quickly in order not to disturb them. With arms clutched around my knees, I gazed at the waves buffeting the rocks just beneath me.

I watched as the myriad bubbles formed the confusion of white surf, before spinning out to create a tracery of patterns on the surface of the water. I became entranced by the spirals, lines and circles that were left behind by the out-going swell. As I stared at the changing shapes in front of me, different images came into my mind with each successive wave that broke. Guruji in his soft wool shawl, John emerging from a cave, Lucas holding his baby sister, and Rachel, Abigail and Charlotte floating out to sea in a boat of light. All came and went, fleeting across my mind like transient dreams. Were they real or illusory? My sister braced herself against the surf, then my father and mother . . . flowers on a hillside, a waterfall and open fells.

As one impression became more dominant, the previous disappeared into the swell of the seas. So many separate images connected by a common thread. And that is me. The storyline. Is it this which continues after death, only to return again and again, to have more images imprinted upon it? When will I awake from this long dream, from this sequence of impressions that makes up me? It exists, yet there is really nothing there. Is life just images, storyline and sea?

Unexpectedly the winds whip up the waves and the images tremble and part. Into the intangible, unknowable presence that lies behind them, I let myself go . . .

Yet the journey never ceases, and the path essentially is pathless . . . But my attitude to it has changed.

I am not driven any more, but rather I am drawn along by an all-enveloping presence that is far greater than me, and knows its course more accurately. This helps me feel secure amidst the turbulence of the ocean waves.

Also by USHA PUBLICATIONS:

THE LIGHT WITHIN

A Celebration of the Spiritual Path

by

John and Eliza Forder

Through a series of inspirational photographs, with accompanying text, poems and prayers, THE LIGHT WITHIN explores many of the ways that people seek spiritual fulfilment today. The story is set against the ethereal beauty of the northern landscape, and celebrates the fact that each one of us has our own way of reaching that inner refuge where peace and fulfilment are found.

For centuries the wildness of the northern landscape has been used to deepen and intensify spiritual experience; nowadays people from varying backgrounds and different faiths are drawn by the rugged splendour of the hills and isles to seek spiritual fulfilment. Whether priest or poet, hill walker or hill shepherd, painter or paraglider, everyone has their own unique way of finding inner peace, yet the ultimate goal is the same – to feel at One – within oneself, within Nature, and with each other.

THE LIGHT WITHIN is a celebration of this multi-faceted approach to the Spiritual Path – it embraces people of all beliefs and lifestyles and helps to increase understanding between faiths.

ISBN   0 9524677 0 4